THE SIKH VISION

Problems of philosophy and faith

Wazir Singh

1992

Ess Ess Publications

ANSARI ROAD, DARYA GANJ
NEW DELHI - 110002

ISBN 81 - 7000 - 137 - 4

First published : 1992
Rs. 150.00

Published by Mrs. Sheel Sethi for Ess Ess Publications,
4837/24, Ansari Road, New Delhi-110002

Printed by : Novelty Process.
E-4/1, Mansrover Park,Delhi-110 032.

PREFACE

The Sikh vision is essentially a philosophic vision of human destiny, inspired by the message of Ten Gurus. The vision encompasses man and his faith in the ground of his being, the Reality Supreme, as also his links with the physical universe and social world. In common with other theistic faiths, the religion of Sikh people presents its view of the Divine and divinity, the Spirit and spirituality, values and virtues, carving out a specific way of life. The medium of scriptural writings being poetry and verse, an appropriate philosophical idiom has to be employed in order to bring out the distinctive character of Sikh thought and culture. The interpretive endeavour followed in the present work, plus other attempts of similar nature, are collectively given the designation of Sikh Philosophy.

Broadly, the discipline of Sikh Philosophy covers the doctrinal aspect of Sikh religion. It comprehends discussion of the metaphysical-cum-cosmological dimension of Sikhism, as also its theory of knowledge and system of values, besides ethical and social philosophy. In fact it is the application of philosophical methodology to the study of Sikh thought that yields the discipline of Sikh philosophy. The approach, evidently, would be rational and analytical, even though the subject-matter necessarily falls in the region of faith and belief. Since it is not philosophy proper, the framework of Sikh Philosophy admits questions that are largely theological, and deals with a body of concepts peculiar to the Sikh faith and tradition. It has to make references to the textual content, which in this case comprises the scripture, *Guru Granth Sahib*, the sacred compositions compiled in the *Dasam Granth*, and the exegetical writings of the savants, scholars and interpreters of Sikhism.

A question has been raised as to the specific title that should be applied to the generic term *Sikh Philosophy*. A section of the work in hand deals with the problem and proposes the title *Akalvada*, i.e. Non-temporalism, for the discipline. *Akaal* is admittedly the most appropriate name applied to the timeless divine Reality of the Sikh vision, and a concept central to the doctrinal framework of Sikhism. The argument has been elaborated with the support of textual references as well as testimony from the Sikh tradition. The concept of Akal also figures in the discussion of the Absolute (*Brahman*), in the section 'The Sikh Vision of God', portraying the Divine in five facets.

Throughout the book, I have underlined the point that the problem of religion, particularly in Sikhism, is *human* problem. If God is praised, it is not for His benefit; if He is remembered, cotemplated or loved, it is for the uplift and edification of man, for the elevation of human spirit to the height divine. The final significance of values too is humanistic in the context of Sikh philosophy and culture. Even the grace of God is for human consumption, for it is man who is blessed, without causing any difference to the nature and status of God the gracious. The focus naturally is on human beings who, of course, look to the Divine for cosmic care and concern in their affairs.

The Sikh way of life rests on the ethico-spiritual teaching enshrined in the sacred lore of Sikhism, and is shaped by the tradition and institutions evolved since the time of Guru Nanak (A.D. 1469-1539). The Sikh vision is obliged to view, besides God and the Divine Ordinance, the problems of knowledge and restructuring of the human faculties, social reality and humanism, suffering and death, all from the Sikh perspective. The cultural life of the Sikh community is rooted in the Punjabi culture. A glance at this aspect of the Sikh life goes to enrich the vision captured in the pages that follow. The purely theological issues involved in the Sikh scenario, are presented from the angle of a noted theologian.

The author expresses his thanks to the editorial boards of reputed journals, such as *The Journal of Religious Studies* (Patiala), *Dialogue and Alliance* (New York), *Studies in Sikhism and Comparative Religion* (New Delhi), for the prior publication of a number of contributions included in *The Sikh Vision*.

The book is dedicated to Professor Henry O. Thompson, University of Pennsylvania at Philadelphia (U.S.A.), in appreciation of his abiding interest in the Sikh thought and praxis.

Wazir Singh

New Delhi
25 February, 1992

THE HOUSE OF GURUS

(Total Period : 240 years)

Guru Nanak occupies the first place in the chronological order of the Gurus. His position and relationship with other Gurus is indicated in the following table :

1. Guru Nank Dev (the First Guru) A.D. 1469-1539 (lifetime : 70 years)
2. Guru Angad (Second Guru) 1504-1552 (48 years). Disciple of Guru Nanak. Guruship : 1539-1552.
3. Guru Amar Das (Third Guru) 1479-1574 (95 years). Disciple of Guru Angad. Guruship : 1552-1574.
4. Guru Ram Das (Fourth Guru) 1534-1581 (47 years). Son-in-law of Guru Amar Das. Guruship : 1574-1581.
5. Guru Arjan Dev (Fifth Guru) 1563-1606 (43 years). Son of Guru Ram Das. Guruship : 1581-1606.
6. Guru Hargobind (Sixth Guru) 1595-1644 (49 years). Son of Guru Arjan Dev. Guruship : 1606-1644.
7. Guru Hari Rai (Seventh Guru) 1630-1661 (31 years). Grandson of Guru Hargobind. Guruship : 1644-1661.
8. Guru Hari Krishan (Eighth Guru) 1656-1664 (8 years). Son of Guru Hari Rai. Guruship : 1661-1664.
9. Guru Tegh Bahadur (Ninth Guru) 1621-1675 (54 years). Son of Guru Hargobind. Guruship : 1664-1675.
10. Guru Gobind Singh (Tenth Guru) 1666-1708 (42 years). Son of Guru Tegh Bahadur. Guruship : 1675-1708.

CONTENTS

THE SIKH VISION OF GOD

God has many names. So has he numerous qualities and attributes. This is true in respect of nearly all the religious traditions called theistic. Sikhism, in line with these faiths, believes in a supreme spiritual Being known by several names, each name standing for a divine attribute posited by the human mind. Names being linguistic symbols, cannot be revealed; they have to be contrived. Attributes may however be intuited, depending upon the conceptual framework adopted. Spiritual mentors (Gurus) of the Sikh religion give expression to their inmost experience of the divine reality with its countless facets and attributes. Their compositions *(Gurbani)*, as a poetic testimony to their inner illumination, offer a fund of names literally running into hundreds, indicating a rich variety of divine functions intuited by them . Each name represents a particular quality, or a specific act performed, and hence is a functional name, with the single exception of *Sat (i)* or *satya*, which in the sense of basic reality or Being as such, is taken to be the primordial name of the Divine.[1]

The functional names of God, from the Sikh point of view, fall into clusters, depending upon their affinity of meaning. These may then be viewed as clusters of attributes revealing various aspects of God. The present study seeks to offer a five-facet scheme of God as viewed in Sikhism.

It may be admitted in the first instance that the thought-structure of Sikhism has a definite metaphysical bias; it presents its basic creed in terms of the features of Supreme Reality of its vision. This depiction has important philosophical, sociological and mystic implications. But, the term God (or its equivalent) as used in *Gurbani*, is not employed in any theological, anthropological or analytical sense. It is decidedly not God talk; nor is it simply a conceptualization. It is the symbolic expression of a believer within the framework of a well-defined tradition. And it is indicative of an inward experience, which by any other name would risk its authenticity. God, thus, remains God, with his five chosen facets, in the present study based upon *Gurbani*.

It may next be conceded that the approach of Sikhism does not give up the rich heritage of Indian philosophy and spirituality. In fact, numerous of its expressions closely resemble the Upanisadic and Advaitic formulations, as well as the Sat-Chit-Anand phraseology, even though its freedom of seeking new orientation and placing new emphases is unmistakable.

The facets of God sought to be discussed in the context of Sikhism, are *facets* of the one underlying reality. Evidently, they are inter-related and must present an integrated view of their subject. In other words, the facets may be seen as dissolving themselves into a coherent system, repeatedly emphasized in the Guru Granth, the Sikh scripture, and other sacred writings including the Dasam Granth (the voluminous collection of spiritual and secular poetry generally attributed to the Tenth Guru). Monotheism as a theological designation may be applicable and has actually been applied, to the Sikh doctrine of God; but it seems more appropriate to apply the philosophical characterization Monism to the absolutistic vision of reality encountered in the Sikh holy writings. Not simply that the Sikhs believe in one God, without the 'other'–that is without owing allegiance to a rival such as the Devil, or to more than one, or a trinity, or a multiplicity of gods. They are also persuaded that, ultimately speaking, all phenomena belong to and merge into one system of reality and *that* is God. It would ot be out of place here to mention that the chief value in the Sikh value-system is Harmony, interpreted as the spiritual merging of the human existence (a drop) into the ocean of Being.

The five facets chosen to portray the Sikh view of divine reality, may conveniently be placed on a scale, in order to form a view of their polar relationships. At one end of the scale we may put the Absolute, and at the other end the Gracious personal God. The three facets, those of the Creator, the Ordainer and the Omniscient would be shown in the middle, in that order.

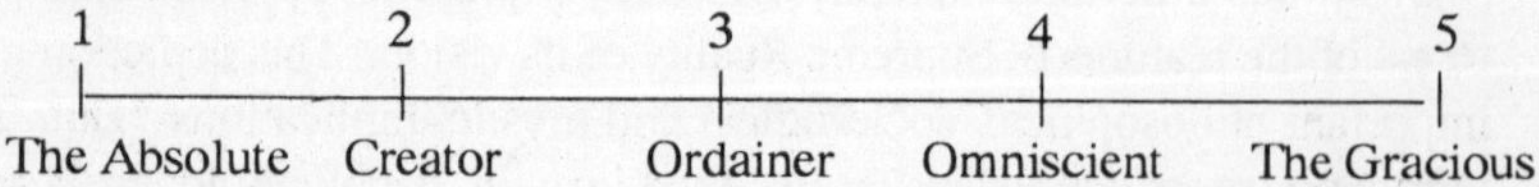

If we read down from the first facet to the fifth one, we notice a hierarchical picture, in as much as the Absolute stands out as the all-encompassing and all-pervasive, transcendent and impersonal undifferentiated Reality. In the second facet, the same very Absolute assumes the character of the Creator, a self-differentiating power whose cosmic framework embodies all that there is, the being and existence of all material, biological and mental phenomena. The third phase portrays the Divine as the Ordainer, whose ordinance prevails in the creation which itself is created by him in his creative aspect. A creator who does not look after his creation, who fails to establish some sort of order and system to maintain what he has brought about, would be like a parent who simply procreates and then abandons the off-spring rightaway. The Divine seems to demonstrate a measure of concern and care unmatched by any of his creatures. This creative and caring God is also the God who knows and understands. This is his fourth dimension, namely his omniscience, which presents him as immanent in all the hearts. This perhaps is the principle of mentality operating in the universe, the 'chit'(*cit*) or consciousness in the traditional triad of Sat-Chit-Anand of Indian philosophy. The final face of God in the scheme is the image of a gracious God, full of tenderness for his creation, full of forgiveness and friendliness, saviour and redeemer, – poet of the world.

On the bi-polar scale indicated above, the facets of impersonal absolute reality and the personal, gracious image of God appear to be poles apart from one another, creating an impression contrary to the one intended. In order to avoid such impression of extremes pulling away from each other, the facets may be plotted on a circle, thereby placing the fifth facet next to the first. Accordingly, the Absolute would be shown as equi-distant from the Creator as well as from the Gracious. Even this circular representation, however, is not an ideal one, since the third facet (Ordainer) and the fourth one (Omniscient) would be seen as further removed from the Absolute as compared with the other two. The hierarchical model, with its distinct advantages, may be retained in some form, but the real import of the whole exercise need not be lost sight of: all the facets are equi-distant from one another, but all belong to the same single reality; rather they collectively portray that reality. The analysis is attempted simply for conceptual convenience in grasping the Sikh approach to the Ultimate.

The Absolute of Sikhism

'Brahman' (pronounced Brahmn) is the name assigned by the Indian philosophical tradition to the all-inclusive, absolute Spirit. It designates the formless, transcendent reality that precedes and pervades all manifestations. This conception of the Supreme Reality, or the Being – Consciousness-Freedom (Sat-Chit-Anand) equivalent of the Brahman, is accepted by Sikhism as its fundamental metaphysical tenet. The entire superstructure of Sikh spirituality stands upon this conception of the Absolute, designated in *Gurbani* by the numeral 1 (one)[2], as also by various other terms such as *Parm-Atman* (the spirit transcendent), *Param-Brahman, Akal Purakh*. The thrust of the basic creed adopted in Sikhism is the affirmation of Being, not its negation. It is no philosophy of nihilism or voidism. Its faith is in the Being that is present, that is one, that is positive. Its Being is not a zero, not a nullity, not nothingness pure and simple.

Apart from the designation of Brahman, the Sikh Gurbani accepts from the Indian tradition the term 'sat' (being), as also 'satya' (reality, truth) commonly written as 'Sat(*i*) in the scriptural text. *Sat*(*i*) is the primordial description of the fundamental reality, all other descriptions being its functional designations. *Sat(i)* is the sole uncontradicted Being admitted in the Sikh faith. All the qualifying attributes of the Supreme Reality can be shown as dimensions with contradictory poles, such as unmanifest: manifest, non-temporal : temporal, infinite : finite, impersonal : personal. (There is no 'non-real entity' – no 'non-being' in Sikh metaphysics.) The apparently contradictory descriptions are polarities, both the polar terms or extremes bearing an internal relationship as if through the axis. For instance, the polarity of non-temporal : temporal dimension of the Ultimate, implies eternality of the Absolute, as well as its immanence in the temporal process of the world emanating from it.

Central to the theme of the Absolute in Sikhism is the concept Akal (timeless) or the non-Temporal. The term *akaal* is used both in the qualifying sense and as a substantive. It may be Akal Murat(*i*), i.e. the timeless image; or it may be Akal, the Timeless. At any rate, the term signifies Reality beyond time, not governed by the temporal process or evolution, and hence Reality eternal. The emphasis placed on the term Akal in the sacred literature of Sikhism, is so pronounced as to make the term percolate to the cultural pattern of the Sikh community. (The highest spiritual-cum-secular seat of the Sikhs is known as Akal Takht, the throne eternal; the popular form of greeting one another among the Sikhs, *Sat Sri Akal*, refers to the everlasting reality of the holy Eternal; and even their dominant political party is known as Akali Dal.) Right from the compositions of Guru Nanak through those of Guru Gobind Singh, the term Akal has been employed with singular stress. So much so, that if a name were to be selected to designate Sikh philosophy (on the lines of Advaitavada of Sankara), no name other than 'Akalvada', i.e. Akalism, would be appropriate enough.

Eternality and temporality (i.e eternity and time) being a polarity, qualify a single reality, with the implication that if the Sumpreme Reality is timeless in one sense, it can be temporal in the other. Both Kal (Time) and Akal (Timeless) have been used in the Dasam-Granth poetry to designate the Spirit Indivisible. The various theistic traditions of the world have dovetailed the timeless and the spaceless, in their depiction of the Divine, as if anticipating the spatio-temporal unity in modern cosmologies. Some of the recent studies distinguish the 'eternal' from the 'everlasting', the latter meaning 'existing within time'. They emphasize Biblical presentation of God as everlasting rather than eternal, even as He is considered the Lord of Time. God is shown as everlasting in the sense that he is steadfast in his redeeming intent.[3] For Sikhism, eternality of God is no anathema to his everlasting nature, or to his temporality in relation to the cosmic order. As 'timeless' he is pure Spirit, that is, without any configuration or form. We cannot form any image of the formless. Yet, in His temporal aspect, He assumes the form of his creation. It is in this sense that the formlessness of God and His cosmic form (*murti*, image) are conjoined in the basic creed of Sikhism.[4] It is a combination of Being-Existence, Unmanifest-Manifest, or the timeless-temporal singularity.

The Absolute of Sikhism has important similarities with the non-dualistic metaphysics of Shankara (viz. Advaitism). Both speak of Brahman as the monistic, spiritual Reality, other than which there is none. Both refer to the world as *maya* (false); but the Maya of Advaita is the grand illusion that is beginningless like Brahman itself; whereas the creation is false, in Sikhism, in the sense of having a beginning and an end in time. The Sikh view, incidentally, resembles the Hegelian model in respect of the Absolute being an all-inclusive, comprehensive, universal Spirit, manifesting itself and shining through all the objects and forms. This cosmic existense or the physical world is but a form of the Absolute, assumed by Itself. The world cannot be completely real, for it is only an aspect, an abstraction, and not the Absolute; it can neither be completely false, – as it is a manifestation of the Real, the True. It partakes the spirituality of the Absolute, even though it appears in its materiality as a partially real entity. The Sikh view of the Absolute clearly emphasizes the spiritual nature of the Supreme Reality and calls it "essence", in contrast with the world of natural order that is "existence". The Essence, on this view, pervades the Existence, thereby lending some of its reality to the world of creation.

The spiritual essence of the Absolute has several implications for the Sikh view of reality. In the first place, only Spirit can be understood as indivisible; a physical object or body is infinitely analysable into progressively smaller bits and particles. The divisiblity of matter leads us to the metaphysical doctrine of absolute pluralism, whereas oneness of the Spirit gives rise to absolutism. Notwithstanding the charm of alternative philosophical theories for the reader, a choice has to be made when it comes to determining the character of a religious belief-system. Sikhism insists highest reality belongs to the spiritual Absolute, which in turn is the source of atomic and sub-atomic entities and their ceaseless series. Analysis is all right; it may even precede synthesis; but it need not debar or shut off the process of synthesis leading to higher and higher unities, like a spiral, finally reaching the Absolute. Another implication of the Sikh spirituality is the potentiality for consciousness embedded in the Absolute, and missing in a purely physical view of reality. The absolute Spirit is not *endowed* with the attribute of awareness, it *is* consciousness, or *chit*, itself. Only a conscious Absolute would be in a position to entertain 'desire' and 'willingness' or to act as the creator and designer of the universe.

The Sikh Gurbani refers to two states of the Absolute: the pre-cosmic, and the cosmic, called the *aphur* and *saphur* states, respectively. In its pre-creation, *aphur* state of desirelessness, the Absolute remains in constant trance, for "ages upon ages," to speak metaphorically. Since there was no existence, no contour or shape, no spatio-temporal form, no process of evolution, the poetic depiction of the 'void' state refers to the "inexpressible, primordial darkess."[5] What prevailed was the divine Will or Ordinance,[6] in the sense of the unique absolute mentality of the Absolute. It is to be noted that the Void of which Guru Nanak speaks, was not devoid of all capability for creation. The Absolute could change into the thought-full, desiring mood (*saphur* state) and cause the processes of creation to work. 'He' would enter into the cosmic phase at will, as if ordering the universe to take shape:

> Initiates He the whole process
> from one sound, one Note,
> And million rivers outflow,
> a million forms float.[7]

Creativity seems to be an outstanding feature of the Absolute, both in the pre-cosmic and cosmic states. When in the pre-creation mood the Absolute is not engaged in the creation-activity, it is all the same endowed with creativity. All creation issues from It, as and when It (i.e.He) so wills. In this sense, the Absolute is the source of all actuality, though in its pre-cosmic stance, it remains an inexhaustible realm of possibility. The impersonal, formless Brahman can hardly be described in human terms; *neti-neti* (not so,not so) of the Unpanisad[8] has been applied to Him by the Tenth Guru. He has repeatedly been called *a-kath* (ineffable) in the Guru-Granth compositions. Yet, since the same very Brahman assumes the status and role of Creator-Person in relation to the cosmic and human orders, some depiction of His nature, some 'expression' of the 'inexpressible' (*a-kath katha*) becomes possible. The mysterious is captured and revealed, commensurate with the seer's insight and gifts.

The Gurus of Sikhism are emphatic about the transcendent nature of the Absolute, who is conceived in terms of the unborn (not cast in the womb), and the un-installed[9] (unlike an image or idol). The eternal Spirit cannot be bound by the spatio-temporal limits; hence no incarnation of the Brahman is conceivable. The transcendent, eternal source of all existence, as depicted in Sikhism, refers to the primordial nature of the Supreme Being (as in Whitehead). His immanence in the cosmic order, however, as believed in Sikhism, accounts for the consequent nature of the Divine. The Absolute (of philosophy) assumes the form of God (of religion). The Sikh view of the dual nature of Absolute-cum-God runs parallel to Shankara's Brahman-Ishvara conception, as well as to the Nirguna-Saguna tradition[10] of Indian philosophy in general

God of Creation

That a supreme, sovereign, all-powerful Being is the author of the world, is as much an article of faith with the followers of Sikhism as with the majority of other religious communities. The facet of God as Creator entails the concept of creation, since it is the function of the creator to create, and perhaps go on creating. Sikhsm differs radically from such philosophical theories as view the cosmic order to be self-existent and remaining in shape for ever. For the naturalist, 'creation' means the coming into existence of the universe as we know it, from an earlier, embryonic stage, sometimes caled the 'cosmic egg'. Alternatively, it may be a 'big-bang' origin of the present form of existence, but the original source of the energy that exploded is not attributed to a divine creator. A religious cosmology, however, is generally inclined to credit God with the establishment of the universe in the finished form, or with the creation of the basic materials that go to constitute it. The divine Being may have brought the world into existence once for all, or may be at work continually to create, destory and re-create at his Will.

The Sikh view of creation equates the created universe with the manifest aspect of the Unmanifest. The formless, spiritual Absolute in its pre-cosmic 'thought-free' phase is the hidden (*gupat*) reality, which in the cosmic 'thought-full' phase assumes the character of revealed (*pargat*) reality.[11] The moment of transformation from the unrevealed to the revealed, from the unmanifest to the manifest, from the impersonal to the personal aspect, is the moment of creation. The pure, shapeless essence turns into cosmic existence, with all its contours and contents, evolutionary process and infinite creative advances. What is potential in one phase becomes actual in the other. The transformation from the realm of possibility into the realm of actuality, is *suo moto,* absolutely free and unconditional. It is not caused by any external pressure, force, or circumstance, for there is nothing 'external' to the Absolute.

This cosmological formulation of the Sikh faith, as adumbrated in the scriptural text, has a number of implications. In the first place, the precise moment of creation remains undefined and mysterious to the human intellect. The motions of the eternal, infinite reality can hardly be known to a temporal, finite being, — at least in the fullest measure. The fathomless, or for that matter, the highest Truth, is not a subject for human knowledge that is always limited, partial and incomplete. As put by Guru Nanak :

> As high as He, one has to be
> One to realize, how high is He![12]

However, there is nothing wrong on the part of humans to endeavour and seek to comprehend, may be gradually or in degrees, the truth of the cosmic order. The epistemology of modern science supports this approach. Moreover, religious mysticism itself hints at the possibility of full revelation of the mysteries of being and existence to the re-moulded and restructured human faculties of intuition and mystic consciousness.

As to the precise moment of earthly time, or the date and day of the first creation, the Sikh belief maintains a posture of silence. Guru Nanak discounts attempts at pin-pointing the time of creation and calls all claims in this respect hollow. The creator alone knows when he creates; He alone knows the extent and measure of his creation.[13] The Sikh cosmology lends itself to more than one interpretation as to the question of origin or coming into being of the world. The creation taking place at one sound or one Note (*kavao*) broadly resembles the Semitic belief, the Creator issuing the commandment (*Kun* : Be!) or saying let there be light. This mode of creating the Universe can be reconciled to the Big-Bang theory of a gigantic explosion billions of years ago. But the expression that the Creator goes on creating endlessly, in Guru Nanak and other Gurus, comes close to the Hindu belief in the periodic creation, as also to the Oscillating or Pulsating Universe theory, with periodic expansions and compressions of the world. A stanza from the Dasam-Granth poetry has an interesting parallel : "When the Creator projects Himself, the world and creatures all take shape; when he draws in and attracts, all embodiments relapse into Him."[14]

Not only that we are unable to determine with a measure of accuracy the age of the 'entire' creation, or even of the current expansion phase of the world, we do not seem to be in a position to determine the nature of Time itself. Did the process of time start with the process of creation, that is, creation of the earth, or of the solar system, or of the galaxy to which 'we' belong, or of the nebulous phase of prime matter, or of the 'cosmic egg'? The question brings into relief the relevance of Guru Nanak's caution to avoid speculation as to the beginning and extent of creation.

How the spiritual Absolute, or insubstantial God, becomes the source of a substantial Universe, remains a puzzle for the theologians. The Sikh view does not claim to offer a final solution : It only states its position, albeit through the medium of poetry. The Absolute in its creative phase is the logical prius of creation that issues forth from it. Such an Absolute, with creative intent, must necessarily be a conscious being and hence 'personal'. The Basic Creed of Sikhism uses the epithet Karta Purakh (Creator-Person) for the divine principle of creation. This expression sounds unique, even though the concept may not be so. The Creator-Person is that facet of the impersonal, un-embodied Absolute which is revered as God. As Creator, God is linked to the creation and the creatures. In the Hindu Trinity, the god Brahma symbolizes the creator-God. In the Sikh cosmology, countless Brahmas (creative forces) are said to reside within the Absolute, all engaged in an endless creative activity. The Creator-Person is one, but his powers and energies are innumerable, and so are the objects emanating from him. The Principle of diversity in unity and unity in diversity is applicable to the Creator-creation relationship.

Along with creativity, the Sikh view refers to numerous other powers inherent in the Divine, making him the Perfect Being, worthy of all the veneration human spirit is capable of. The 'perfection' of omnipotent God is alluded to again and again in the textual compositions. As Perfect Being, he indwells in his creation and delights in his own deed. As the sovereign creative power, He creates as He likes, and is perfectly free. His blissful state (Anand) is rightly interpreted as Freedom. In the Basic Creed of Sikhism, the symbol *Nirbhau* (lit. fearless) stands for the sovereignty and joy of the Divine, who is without an authority over him or superior to him. He, the Spirit, installs Himself, assuming the form of natural order; and He the ultimate ground of all that is, sustains and ordains his creation with loving care and delight.

God, the Ordainer

Among the key-concepts of Sikh spirituality is the divine Ordinance, *Hukam*, that ranks in the philosophic hierarchy of Sikhism next only to Akal (the Timeless) and Karta (Creator). 'Hukam' and its derivative 'Hukami' (Ordainer) stand, respectively, for the ordinance that prevails in the cosmic existence and the divine source from which the ordinance issues. Sikhism firmly believes that the Universe is maintained as a systematic, disciplined and ordered whole by the Omnipotent Creator who is also the Lord of his creation. The terms 'Onkar (Oamkaar) occurring in the Basic Creed and eleswhere in *Gurbani,* signifies the divine Being intimately associated with the world as its creator and protector. He is the Providence; He is the sustenance and support of the created order. As Hukami, the sovereign divine Person, it is His Writ that prevails, and his creatures have no option but to submit to his Will. As Guru Nanak clearly states in the *Japuji* – "All are governed by the Ordinance Divine, none outside its pale; he who recognizes the Ordinance, Nanak, never shall assert his ego again."[15]

In a sense, the divine Ordinance implies the truth of existence which is gradually and progressively discovered by man, in the form of the laws of Nature. As the men of science probe the different levels of natural order, they find more and more evidence of orderliness and design, in the physico-chemical, biological and psycho-social spheres of existence. Nobody seriously questions the fact of "at least some degree of order as well as a wide variety of ordered arrangements of physical reality." "Sheer indeterminateness is nothingness. To be actual is to be something definite, and this implies being ordered."[16] The question is whether an ultimate principle of order, viz. God, can be scientifically reconciled with the orderliness of nature. Science with its own parameters, refuses to venture into speculation,–a territory fondly held by philosophy and theology. Not surprising therefore that the issues of divine existence, divine will, and divine purpose are generally precluded from the scope of science. It is another matter that "scientists of the stature of Einstein, though they reject traditional ideas of God, have called for a religious response of wonder and awe in the face of cosmic mysteries."[17] Sikhism responds with faith, not only to the mystery of the Universe, but to the divine origin of all mystery.

Apart from order experienced in nature, there are questions of purpose and novelty closely linked with the problem of natural order. The term 'cosmos' itself implies that we believe in the existence of an ordered universe, and not in 'chaos'. The fact of the solar system and lunar motions following a pattern, was known to the ancient man as it is known to the modern man. The Sikh religious texts, too, make references to the elements and streams, angels, and seers, the sun and the moon, all performing their assigned roles under the discipline of the supreme Ordainer. As for purpose, the position is not simple, since unlike order, the purpose, if any, involved in the cosmos, is not evident to the human common sense or science. Sikhism, not indulging in the speculative teleology of philosophers, however, has implicit faith in the existence of a divine purpose in the cosmic operations. Rather, the entire creation, including humanity, is seen as fulfilling the purpose for which it was originally established. What precisely that purpose is, is known only to the Divine.

Philosophers, since Aristotle, have posited some sort of 'final cause' or purpose for which a thing is made. Recent thinkers have proposed 'formative causation'–as distinct from the mechanical cause producing an effect,–with the implication that something is 'pulling' from in front, contrary to the 'push' from behind. Those who read a cosmic purpose in the world, postulate the emergence of a new world every moment, in its march towards the final goal. The Sikh doctrine is sympathetic to such view and speaks of the progressive renewal of the world, as also of the Master (*Sahib*) himself "who is newer everyday."[18] The Ordainer is the source of order as well as novelty in the cosmic existence. The suggestion of Whitehead in respect of "the world's creative advance into novelty" may well be assimilated to this belief.

The facet of God the Ordainer in Sikhism, besides being the Provident and Protector, as well as the prime source of order, novelty and purpose, is also the facet of an autonomous Lord, rather the principle of Freedom. The traditional Indian figure of 'lila' (playfulness), employed in Sikh *Gurbani* endorses the freedom aspect of the Ordainer. He designs and re-designs the world according to his own choice. All life and death, production and consumption, good and evil in the world, follow his motions and will, which remains a mystery to his creatures. One is not to apportion blame to the divine Ordainer for the existence of evil: for all we know, it may all be part of the mysterious Design. Guru Nanak avers in the Japuji, numerous people constantly live in suffering and misery, but this again may be the gift of the Bounteous One, whose ways are inscrutable.[19]

God, the Omniscient

The dimension of Omniscience is the fourth facet of God in the present study. Divine omniscience is interpreted to mean all things are present to God : His knowing is from eternity. Nothing is concealed from his Vision. In other words, Omniscience is part of God's 'essence'- which implies that no human action can be truly voluntary.[20] The epithet 'antaryami', traditionally applied to the Divine, and freely used in *Gurbani*, brings into focus God's consciousness of what goes on in the human mind, that is, in the mind of each and every individual. This attribute of mentality is what constitutes the 'personality' of God, since it is essentially the consciousness that is the core of a person. The absolute Spirit as the formless, impersonal reality, is not devoid of mentality or *chit*; but in spite of its spirituality, it is treated as impersonal, i.e.without the 'thought' of creation (in the pre-cosmic, *aphur* state). The character of thoughtfulness transforms the Absolute into the God of creation and sustenance, God of knowledge and grace.

The characteristic of all-knowledge or omniscience does not 'belong' to the divine Being; in other words, *chit* (consciousness) is not 'in' the *Sat-Chit-Anand* Absolute; the Absolute 'is' *chit* itself, just as it 'is' *anand* (delight, freedom) itself. To put it differently, the divine Being is the principle of all consciousness and thinking, all reason and wisdom. His light (*jyoti*) lights up all lights in the world: He enlightens all his creatures.[21] The Sikh scripure has reserved the symbol *Gur* (or *guru*, enlightener) for the omniscient Divine. Man's rationality has its prime source in His Reason. As put by Whitehead, " No reason can be given for the nature of God, because that nature is the ground of rationality."[22] Without the prime Reason, the world would really be an absurd world, a chaotic world, if at all. The existentialists who consider the human world an absurdity, do so because they find God as the principle of rationality missing from the world. An absolute 'thinking' Spirit is the necessary condition of all human ratiocination.

Knowledge of God is not limited to knowledge of his creation and creatures alone. It is knowledge of Himself as well. "Thy notions are known to Thee." Or, as Hegel said "God is God insofar as He knows Himself. His self-knowledge is, further, man's self-consciousness and the human knowledge of God, which moves on so as to become one's self knowledge in God."[23] This does not mean, however, that human knowledge is on the same footing as God's knowledge. Man partakes only partially in the rational and other 'powers' of God. *Gurbani* treats man as little–knowing *(alpagya)* as compared with all-knowing (*sarbagya*) God. The character of ineffability in respect of God implies the human inability to know the motions of God in full measure, and to express them adequately. Practically all the mystics the world over have described the Ulitmate as ineffable, i.e. non-conceptualizable. Sikhism is not at variance with this assertion.

The issue of ineffability gives rise to problems such as man's faith and the Divine-human relationship in general. Faith may imply "a relation *between* the Divine and the human, in which the Divine is both other than the human and yet inwardly related to it.[24] In the present age of science, thinkers have raised the question whether scientific knowing is the only legitimate mode of knowing. They tend to regard faith as a mode of consciousness whereby we open ourselves to being grasped by a more comprehensive dimension of reality than the mind itself can objectively master.''[25] To the man of faith, God descends with His light and enlightens his soul, – that is the belief inculcated by the Sikhs. Hegel's categorical assertion—"No finite mind can fully grasp, and no finite language can adequately express, the Absolute," - clinches the issue. Hegel's view of God's "absolute knowlege" might best be described as "Faith above faith."[26] Both faith and reason being human faculties in quest for Truth, the relation between the two is not of separation but of fusion.

Sikhism believes that the Omniscient divine Being is responsive to the urgings of his creatures. He as the focus of loyalty for the devotees, acts as Lord (*Ishvar*) unto them. If the Supreme Being were incapable of 'listening to' their prayers or 'knowing' their state of being, He would not be worthy of the devotion of the devotees. It is the facet of 'all-knowing' Absolute-God that is depicted as *antaryami* and whom the man of faith knows in his inmost experience. The *bhagats* (loving devotees of God) enjoy His presence in them and before them. The *gyanis* (philosophic seekers) have all their doubts dispelled and all their inquiries answered. A true Sikh (lit. disciple) is the one who not only 'knows' but 'enjoys' his God. He is a believer in the spiritual presence of the infinite Being all around, – an element of universal mentality, or feeling, or prehension, in the idealistic metaphysics of Sikhism. At the level of religious faith, this spirituality assumes the form of an omniscient Being who knows the state of his people, who decides the fate of his worldly beings, and indeed the destiny of the human race.

The Gracious God

The God of Grace is the facet of committed God. His commitment is catering for the needs of his creation as Providence, understanding the aspirations of his creatures as Omniscient, and redeeming his people in his graciousness. The sacred texts have several names for the gracious Lord. He is god of mercy and compassion (*daya*), full of parental tenderness and care (*pita* and *mata*), associate and friend (*mitr, sakha*), generous and bounteous (*datar*), God of blessings and graces (*meharvan, kripa-sarup*). As creator, God is obliged by his nature to protect, nurture and love the beings he creates. Sikhism is one with most of other theistic faiths in designating the Divine as God of love (*Prem*), even identifying him with love. In the Divine-human relationship , the devotee loves his Lord, and the latter responds with love to his devotee.

The first demonstration of God's grace, as evidenced in scriptures, is the gifts he bestows upon the world and humanity. Creation itself is a blessing emanating from the creativity of the Absolute. For the earthly creatures, physical conditions supporting life, provision of air, water in abdunance, and the spark of intelligence by which to flourish and move forward, are all among the countless blessings gifted by the Creator-Person in his act of grace. In God we find "the bounty of food for eyes, mind, ears, and stomachs. God's gift to us is this life, this world, this creation." So says Elizabeth Gray.[27] Christian scholars interpret God's gracious gifts in terms of the biblical Covenant, recently designated 'The Cosmic Covenant' by Henry Thompson. "God has a relationship with nature," he says. "God has a covenant with nature." "He is the Creator who very clearly controls in his Omnipotent power that which he has created." "Both history and creation stand under the providence of God" who has "continued in a covenant of grace with mankind."[28]

The concept of Grace , diffcult to reconcile with the Hindu doctrine of Karma, nevertheless finds mention in the Indian characterization of God as *Kripa* and *Prasadi*, verbal equivalents of Semitic Karm and Mehar. Both sets of epithets, with a host of other formations, are employed as attributive names of the Divine, in the Sikh hymns. *Prasad(i)* (Grace) occurs in the Basic Creed itself, where it is interpreted variously as Invocation to the One Absolute Spirit by whose grace the text is composed; or as referring to the Guru by whose grace the Supreme Reality is realized; or reality itself whose essence is Grace. The Tenth Guru, at the outset of his reverential homage to the divine (in his *Jaap*), calls him Akal

(Eternal) and Kripal (the Gracious).[29] Here is a specimen of polarity of the Impersonal and the Personal in Sikh thought. As non-temporal Absolute, the Ultimate transcends all that we know; as Immanent spiritual Being, he is identical with the temporal creation sustained and maintained by him.

In his intimate relation with the temporal world, God the gracious is depicted as "suffering in the sufferings of his people," as well as "sharing in the happiness of the men of piety." The biblical God, too, is represented in a similar fashion. "The God we know is a suffering God, a heart broken God. No one has suffered more throughout history than God."[30] The Sikh view accepts the fact of suffering and evil in the world as part of the divine scheme; a blessing in disguise, as it were. And, God in his grace knows how and when to redeem his people. His grace is the element of cosmic concern in the affairs of humanity confined to this earthly life. His grace, again, is the principle and source of all graciousness in the lives of men. "God's relation to or his concern for humanity is always ethical. In this sense, the very nature of the relationship carries obligations."[31] No wonder that the Sikh view of God is that of a God of Virtue, a God of Ethics.

Guru Arjan, the Fifth spiritual mentor, defines the loftiest 'religion' in terms of - "Contemplation of the Divine Being, and performance of Virtuous Act."[32] The life of spirit, in this human world, is interwoven with a life of morality: "No devotion is complete without the moral deeds," says Guru Nanak, adding :[33]

> All hail to primal Source, the sole Creator,
> Power! He is Truth, he Beauty
> Spirit's joy for ever.

NOTES

1. Distinction between the primordial name and functional names of God is made in passages in the *Guru Granth* (e.g. p. 1083) and the *Dasam Granth*, opening hymn.
2. The *Guru Granth* opens with the numeral '1' (one) signifying affirmation of one single reality. It is followed by a dozen or so qualifiers,constituting the *Mul-Mantra* or the Basic Creed of Sikhism.
3. See N. Wolter Storff, ''God Everlasting'' in Steven Cahn and David Shatz (Eds), *Contemporary Philosophy of Religion,* New York : Oxford University Press, 1982, p.83.
4. *Mul-Mantra,* placed at the head of the *Guru Granth*; also as the invocation hymn of 'Japuji'.

5. *Maru Solhe* (Guru Granth, pp. 1020-43) containing cosmological formulations by Guru Nanak.
6. Ibid.
7. Japuji (G.G.,p.7). See *The Sikh Prayer* (Series one), Ed. Wazir Singh, 1982.
8. Brihadaranyaka Upanisad, iv. 2,4; see J.N.Farquhar, *The Crown of Hinduism*, 1913 (1971), p.229.
9. Japuji (*Guru Granth*, p.1); repeated numerously.
10. See Pratima Bowes, *The Hindu Religious Trandition*, 1976, p.201.
11. *Maru Solhe*, op. cit.
12. *The Sikh Prayer*, op. cit., p.23.
13. Ibid. p.21.
14. *Dasam Granth* (Benati Chaupayi composition).
15. Japuji, op. cit.
16. John F. Haught, *The Cosmic Adventure*, Paulist Press, 1984, pp.83-4.
17. Ibid., p.95.
18. *Guru Granth*, p.660.
19. Japuji, op. cit.
20. Cf. Nelson Pike, "Divine Omniscience and Voluntary Action" in Cahn and Shatz, op. cit.
21. *Guru Granth*, p.663.
22. *Science and the Modern World*, p.249.
23. *Philosophy of Mind*, Part 3 of *The Encyclopaedia*.
24. R.K.Williamson, *Introduction to Hegel's Philosophy of Religion*, Albany, 1984, p.296.
25. Cf. John Haught, op.cit.
26. Cf. Williamson, op.cit., p.301.
27. See "The Cosmic Covenant", Henry O.Thompson (Ed.), *The Global Congress of the World's Religions*, 1982, p.332.
28. Ibid., pp.330-43.
29. *Dasam Granth*, Jaap, stanza 2.
30. John A. Sonneborn in Henry O. Thompson (Ed.), *Unity in Diversity*, New York, 1984, p.208.
31. Henry Thompson, *Global Congress*, op.cit., p.354.
32. Sukhmani, *Guru Granth*, p.266.
33. Japuji, *The Sikh Prayer*, op.cit., p.21.

THE LOVE OF GOD IN SIKHISM

Notionally, the love of God on the part of man, has to be distinguished from God's love for man, even though the two constitute a polarity, particularly in the Sikh faith. The goal of life, in Sikhism, is union with God. But, "this union demands some distinction of God and man, in which relationship can flourish."[1] The union is not absolute identity. "The difference between communion and identity is essential for an understanding of mystical religion,"[2] that Sikhism is believed to be. In this''I-Thou" relationship of love between man and God, the pole of human love is expressed in terms of loving devotion, and the other pole, of God's love for man, in terms of his Grace. "He who knows God dwells undisturbed in the love of God; God abides eternally with the man who knows God."[3] Knowing God, in Sikhism, is not simply a cognitive process; it is enjoying the Divine presence in one's being, that is, an ecstatic experience of the aesthetico-spiritual realm, symbolized by *wismad* and *anand* (ecstasy and bliss).

The Subject -Object of Love

From the human angle, the subject of love is man and the object, God, whereas from the Divine angle, it is other way round. In the I-Thou relationship, the "I" shifts its position from the human end to the Divine end when love is seen flowing from God towards man. Love gives joy to both the lover and the beloved; joy is maximum when it relates two human beings in mutual love. "So also the joy experienced by God is potentially greatest when the object of His love most nearly resembles Him.''[4] As Chung Hwan Kwak observes: ''Love is fundamentally important as the basis of all true relaltionships." He argues that "the creation follows from God's desire to seek joy through sharing His love," and "Jesus did not love abstractly, in vacuum. He loved real human beings. Joy arises only when the lover has a beloved to love."[5] This nearly sums up the Sikh position on the subject-object of love. Guru Nanak repeatedly asserts that the Creator cherishes His creation in utmost joy; He casts loving glances on his earthly beings.[6]

But, in Sikhism, God in His personal dimension is not the sole reality. Guru Nanak and his successor-Gurus talk in terms of the non-personal, non-temporal, absolute Spirit as the other facet of the Supreme Reality. This has the backing of India's spiritualistic tradition, epitomized in Tagore's view. "He calls Reality *advaitam* (non-dual) in which love plays a dominant role." But, Tagore maintains that "Love is backed by *gnosis*. Love, therefore, leads the seeker to merging in the Absolute." "Love, for Tagore, accomplishes the same goal as knowledge does. Both aim at identity by transcending the world of duality. Love, in this sense, is meditative and intuitive".[7] Mahatma Gandhi substitues *gnosis* with Truth. He puts 'love' into his philosophy "by making Truth accessible by love. Truth for him is not only God but also Love." Both Tagore and Gandhi point in the same direction when, like the Gurus of Sikhism, they combine realization in Action with realization in Love; being essentially the same, both "lift man beyond his ego to the path towards the realization of the Infinte.''[8]

Love as experience of joy and love leading to gnosis and holy communion are the themes of theoligical and philosophical writings the world over. In his day, Augustine portrayed love as an impulse to union through dominance. His concept of love was a "kind of life coupling, or seeking to couple, the lover with the object of his love." He insisted that "it was only by self-surrender that one offered visible proofs of invisible loving, or that, in a knitting together of hearts, the 'I' could be perfected in the love of the 'you'.''[9] Much earlier, Plato spoke of a "natural attraction of the imperfect towards its perfect self. A lover is seeking the other half of himself which can only be the good." According to Plato, "all the quests and conflicts of this life are stirred up by love for immortality."[10] Aristotle, for whom the artist was present in the work of art, conceded the dependence of the Creator upon his creation.[11] God is not only an 'artist' at work but Poet of the world with his heart throbbing with the throbs of fellow humans. Herein lies the joy of love experienced by the Divine as subject, in relation to man as the object.

Karl Morrison, in referring to John Donne's *Meditations*, remarks that since God inhabits all things, God and the world are, in some sense, identical. Donne's epistemology was expressed in ''the identity between knower and the known (or subject and object),''[12] implying the identity of lover and beloved, artist and work, and so on. Sikhism depicts this identity as between the *bhakta* (loving devotee) and *Prabhu* (the gracious Lord). The scriptural texts of Sikhism are full of references to this love-relation, which is essentially a spiritual experience of union in the deepest caves of the human heart. Guru Gobind Singh, the tenth embodiment of the Nanak Spirit, in one of his better-known verses, represents the Sikh approach thus:

Listen all of You,
I proclaim the truth:
They alone realize the Lord
Who tread the path of Love.[13]

Ecstasy of Divine Love

The thirty-six poet-philosophers of the Guru Granth and numerous authors, exponents and interpreters of Sikhism, give expression to the appealing qualities of the God of their fancy and imagination, at the same time sharing their conception of the transcendent Reality that is without a quality or attribute. The doctrine of an immanent-transcendent Supreme Being, at once personal and impersonal, temporal yet timeless, essentially one but existentially many, infinite and formless yet present in all finite forms, – is part of Sikh metaphysics. The Sikh prayer is addressed to the Absolute-God who is beyond all prayer, yet as the Lord of creation listens to human prayers and beseechments, and responds with His acts of Grace. The bhakta–Prabhu relationship, depicted colourfully and repeated innumeralbly in the Sikh religious literature, identifies the personal, attributed aspect of the Divine. He is the Beloved Master, Parent, and Friend to the devotee. He is praised not only for the gifts and boons He bestows upon humanity, but also for His 'sweet' temper and tone, His likeable ways, His 'impressive' eyes and 'lovely' teeth, 'beautiful' nose and 'long' tufts of hair.[14] Sheikh Farid , a Sufi contributor of the Guru Granth, counts several sweet objects, viz. sugar, jaggerry, candy, honey and milk, but none would compare his Lord in sweetness.[15]

A major source of ecstasy for the loving devotees has been their mysterious relationship with the Lord-Spouse, in what is termed 'spiritual marriage' in Christianity and Sikhism alike. Just as Christian mystics have spoken of the soul-bride participating in the divine life, taking God as the Bridegroom, the symbolism of wife-husband love-relation has been employed in the poetic compositions of the Gurus. The Indian tradition of marriage involves four to seven circlings by the bride-bridegroom pair, round the sacred fire, *vedi* or the holy Book, at the time of wedding. These circumambulations were adopted as the motif for the spriritual nuptials in the verses known as Lavan, by Guru Ram Das.[16] The four stanzas of this composition are recited and sung at the wedding ceremony of Sikh couples, suggesting that human bonding in marriage is the ground for the soul's surrender unto the Divine embrace. Generally speaking, Eastern mystics of all traditions use the language and imagery of sexual love in their expression of the experience of union.[17] But, the intensity of love depicted in the Guru-Granth verses is a class by itself. "The human soul is a female," and God the male to be wooed. The soul "wins Him by its chastity and total surrender. The Lord comes to its door." "The spiritual love, according to the Gurus, was only concentration of our total being in love."[18]

St. John of the Cross highlights the importance given to love in the 'new life' by calling the renewed person 'the bride of Christ'. "He terms the higher state of the new life 'the state of the spiritual betrothal' and the highest state 'the spiritual marriage.'" Going a step further, the Saint compares the experience of such love "to the flames that rise from a furnace when the fire within it is stirred."[19] In the Taoist and Tantric art-forms, the act of sexual union is portrayed, in the belief that the human act of love re-enacts the sacred marriage of heaven and earth. "Mystical writers often use sex as an image to express their mystical exprience. The soul is identified with the woman. The experience is private and personal, joyful, receptive and ecstatic."[20] For Anders Nygren, "Agape is patterned on Divine love," for it is unselfish, and 'sacrificial giving', unlike Eros that is patterned on 'acquisitive' and 'egocentric love'. The Sufi poetess Rabia, however, makes it clear that "love towards God is qualitatively different from any other kind of love."[21] In the Hindu tradition of *bhakti*, the personal devotion and love of God takes on five 'flavours': quiet contemplation, active service, friendship, filial attachment and passionate love, leading to loss of self in rapture. In return there is love of God for man, because, *Gita* says, "you are very dear to me," "keep me in your thoughts, worship me, sacrifice to me, honour me," and "I will tell you your salvation."[22]

The uniqueness of Guru-Granth poetry lies in its nobility and sublimity. "Here the romanticism is transmuted into the passion for God."[23] Even if the analogy of romantic poetry is used, the orientation remains aesthetic and spiritual. Through the lyrical device of depicting the beloved's pain of separation, and ecstatic joy of union, the sublime path of spiritual ascent is clearly indicated. In Professor Talib's translation, some of the verses read:

> Joy-filled is my heart, blossoming with holy truth;
> Charmed am I by His love –
> Love of the eternal Lord.[24]
> The Lord who has decked the bride
> will also confer his love;

In union with Him lies joy.
The Spouse's embrace blesses the bridal couch...
She who has love of the Divine Spouse night and day,
Is of eternally blessed matrimony.[25]
As the fish lives not out of water;...
As the humming-bee seeking the flower's
 trapped fragrance gets trapped—
Even such in the devotees is love for God:
In His sight alone they find fulfilment.[26]
In devotion are my eyes drenched in *amrita* (nectar)
My heart dyed in love...
Lord God! Thy words of Divine love
 have shot at my heart
With their barbed arrows.[27]

Variety of Love-experience

The Sikh religious poetry presents a remarkable variety of love experience. Depending upon the mood of the poet, the expression of love for God takes on a distinct form, appropriate to the given mood, even if at bottom the spirit of loving devotion be the same. The most outstanding poet of the Sikh lore is Guru Nanak himself. "He sang the songs of Divine love. Out of the fullness of heart flowed his mesage – the message of love of God, the message of brotherhood of man and the law of love in all human relations."[28] In this context, A. R. Wadia observes: "After going through the songs of Guru Nanak, one gets the impression that he was truly God-intoxicated even more than Spinoza was in Europe."[29] Sometimes the degree of 'intoxication' is so overpowering, the poet appears an eccentric to people at large. "Smitten with the love of God, the world takes him to be a madman. He is love-filled, love-intoxicated and God-possessed."[30] In one of his captivating hymns, Guru Nanak alludes to such misconception about his own state, on the part of onlookers who use epithets like eccentric and crazy for him.[31]

If the experience and enjoyment of love turns a minstrel of divine songs into an 'eccentric', or gives him the feeling of being a 'spouse' of the Lord, at times it also strikes him with a heightened sense of wonder. The Guru Granth poetry is strewn with paradoxical metaphors portraying the unicity as well a diversity of Reality. The most notable instance is available in the *Arti* hymn of Guru Nanak, which in part reads: "Thousands are Thine eyes/And yet Thou hast no eyes/Thousands are Thy shapes/And yet Thou hast no shape/Thousands are Thy pure feet/And yet Thou hast not one foot/Thousands are Thy noses/And yet Thou hast no nose./All this is Thy play and bewitches me."[32] We see and have lights in our lives, but perhaps it is one divine Light that lights all the lamps and shines forth through them. In reference to Gerhoch of the twelfth-century Reichersberg, Karl Morrison has drawn a parallel: "There were many books, but one Scripture, written by one Spirit and so rightly considered one book; many churches but one Church; and many heavens, but one Heaven."[33]

Mutuality of love between man and God is another experience treated at many levels in the Guru-Granth compositions. Sheikh Farid, for whom 'greed is the negation of love', portrays his God as "sweet, loving, compassionate, provident, master, magnanimous and beloved." All the pleasant comforts of life may be sacrificed for the sake of such sweet Lord - "I fear not the loss of youth/If love of God be retained/O Farid, countless youthful looks/For want of love have withered away."[34] The metaphor employed by Farid suggests as if God were in physical contact with man. It is a kind of love that, in its widest meaning, has been described as simply an "intense, positive interest in an object," by Smiley Blanton. "When we love a thing, we become deeply engrossed in it with all our senses. This is true whether the thing we love is a woman or a flower, a food or a landscape, a song or a philosophical theory. In each case we want to come into closest contact with it - to look at at, touch it, listen to it."[35] Indeed, we cannot know and understand a thing by adopting an attitude of hostility towards it.

But, the subtlety of love as 'nameless experience' transcends all mundane connections. As the 'lonely wayfarer' J. Krishnamurti records his mystical state: "I have seen the glorious and healing Light. Love in all its glory has intoxicated my heart; my heart can never be closed. I have drunk at the fountain of Joy and eternal Beauty."[36] Sikh spirituality, at its height, touches these deeper levels of human personality, of which the Indian tradition speaks in terms of the Atman. "It is the discovery of the *atman* that made for the message of peace, harmony, universal love and cooperation."[37] The recipients of divine love in their *atman* are 'the elect' (literally, the *panch*) in Guru Nanak's Japuji. In a remarkable similarity of expression, Augustine affirms: "Through the Holy Spirit, God diffused a greater than human love in the hearts of the elect."[38] Endowed with such blessing, they adorn the highest pedestals in the Divine Court. In the words of Guru Nanak:

> The Elect win approval, the Elect prominence,
> The Elect receive honours in divine Audience.[39]

In order to attain to the level of the elect or *panch*, one has to be worthy of the Divine grace. But, as the Gurus caution, blessings are all in the hands of the Master who cannot be coaxed or forced to part with any. The only way open to man qua man, is self-surrender, or resigning oneself to the Will divine through the act of contemplation. Guru Gobind Singh has very emphatically discounted the ritualistic devices and postures conventionally prescribed for winning godly favours. One of his hymns, in Gopal Singh's translation, reads:

> Without loving devotion, nothing avails,
> Neither vast sacrificial fires, nor *yagnas*,
> nor customary charities.
> Without single-minded devotion to the Name of One God,
> All religious effort ends in fruitlessness.[40]

Though in the final analysis, even devotion and meditation are determined by God's Grace, the Sikh spirituality commends honest effort in seeking a qualitative enrichment of one's being. Unflinching faith in the teaching of the Guru Granth, is prescribed as the disciple's pathway to salvation, attainable in this very human life. Love and service of God is one part of the prescription; love and service of humanity is the other, complementary part.

Love of God : Love of Man

Love, in its theistic as well as humanistic dimensions, is one of the intrinsic values in the Sikh axiology. Without love of God and without love of man, no hierarchy of Sikh values can be constructed. Both the dimensions find their illustration in numerous passages of the scriptural text. Says Guru Nanak:

> Listen My heart:
> Let thy love be that of the lotus for the pool,
> Though the ripples shake the lotus and torment it,
> It flowers and loves even more the waters...
> Listen, my heart: love God ceaselessly
> As the fish loves water...
> O my heart, listen:
> Love God as water loves milk.
> The water must suffer, must evaporate
> Before the heat can touch the milk.[41]

From the Sikh point of view, love is not that which endures not, nor is it that which is transferred to another one. Constancy of love is what is most highly prized.

Another point of note is that love is defined in Sikhism as a union of the souls, for a "union of the bodies is no union." Guru Amar Das insists: "They are not truly husband and wife/Whose bodies merely come together/Only they are truly wedded/When two bodies have one soul."[42] The analogy is a pointer to the union of the human and the divine, through enduring love. Assertion of one's ego hampers the realization of divine love. As the 'cobbler saint' Ravidas puts it so succintly: When "I" am/"You" are not/Now that my "I" is no more/"You" alone are."[43] This is precisely what self surrender means in the Sikh faith. The regenerated individuals, "the elect", are the emancipated ones, that is, those liberated from the shackles of egoism. They enjoy the unchartered freedom of moving from one realm to the other, from the domain of temporal life to that of the spiritual life, as and when they will.

The Sikh conception of the Divine portrays the latter as immanent in the living beings of this world. In the words of Guru Arjan (as addressed to Sheikh Farid),[44] "the Provident is present in the people, the people have their being in God." Here the Sikh view runs parallel to the Biblical affirmation: "He is not afar from any of us: For in Him we live and move and have our being" (Acts 17:27-28). The Christian belief that love of God and of neighbour is same, when properly assimilated, brings home the message of the "interanimation of love by which soul flows into soul, and the interassurance of the mind by which two loving souls are one, even when lovers part." The sentiment (paraphrased from John Donne)[45] is echoed by exponents of other faiths. K. A. Nizami avers : "Muslim mysticism is, in its essence, a message of love. It aims at creating harmony in the discordant elements of society."[46] Baba Farid, with a heart overflowing with Divine love, strove to create an atmosphere of love, faith, tolerance and sympathy, not different from the Christian spirit of charity, or from the Sikh prayer for the 'well-being of all .

Love of man finds its natural and immediate expression within the family circle. Founders of Shinto, in Japan, saw love rooted in the family. So much so, that "the most profound and powerful emotion of the Japanese is grateful and reverential love for the dead," forming the basis of their patriotism, filial piety and loyalty.[47] The Sinto teaching eventually leads to the motto 'All men are brothers' that sounds Gandhian in its formulation. When Swami Vivekananda attended Parliament of Religions (Chicago, 1893), and addressed the audience as 'Sisters and Brothers of America', " the effect was electrical; the whole audience stood up to a man cheering and waving wildly for minutes."[48] Even Feuerbach invested some elements of theology in his materialist doctrines of society when he said - "The being of the other is my being." An individual man was only man, but "man with man - the unity of I and you - is God." "In loving, I bind my being to the being of another; I exist only in the other, with the other, and for the other. Not loving, I exist only for myself."[49] No wonder, the message of human harmony and harmonious unity is sponsored by philosophers and religious leaders alike.

Motoori Norinaga, a Shinto thinker of the eighteenth-century Japan, defines virtue and goodness in terms of sympathetic kindness and awareness of the sorrow of human existence. "His idal man is the authentic human being who is neither afraid nor ashamed to feel and behave like a human being." "He has no hope of *nirvana* or a happy life after death, but to the extent possible he hopes to find happiness and enjoy beauty and love here and now, though not uninterruptedly."[50] Both the idea and the idiom used by Motoori are modernistic. Guru Nanak who predates him, presents the picture of the ideal man and ideal society in terms equally relevant to the spirit of contemporary era. His successors and associates underlined his emphasis on the transformed and regenerate man whom they called 'gurmukh' - one who is both God-oriented and humanistically inclined, who endeavours to put love where it is missing, who believes in sharing rather than keeping within the pearls of spirituality. To them love of God was not an abstraction, not merely a notion or conviction, but a genuine, transparent spirit of service and dedication. For them, all men are humans, without distinctions of race, colour or caste. Guru Gobind Singh's declaration - "I recognize the entire humanity as one single race"[51] - is concise, timely and most valuable for us, the *homo sapiens*.

NOTES

1. Geoffrey Parrinder, 'The Nature of God,' in Harbans Singh (Ed.), *Perspectives on Guru Nanak*, Patiala: Punjabi University, 1975, p.91.
2. Ibid., p.87.
3. Ibid., p.87 (quotation from Guru Arjan's Sukhmani', *Adi-Granth*, p.273).
4. Chung Hwan Kwak, 'God and Creation in Unification Theology', in Sontag & Bryant (Eds.) *God : The Contemporary Discussion*, New York : The Rose of Sharon Press, 1982, p.88.
5. Ibid., pp.88-89.
6. Cf. Guru Nanak's 'Japuji' and Var Asa, *Adi-Granth*, pp. 8, 463.
7. Kapil Tiwari, 'God : A Contemporary Indian Discussion', in *God*, op.cit., pp.252-3.
8. Ibid., pp.250-52.

9. Karl F. Morrison, *I Am You,* Princeton University Press, 1988, 00.147, 152.
10. Ibid, pp. 12-13.
11. Ibid., p.21.
12. Ibid., p.26.
13. *Dasam Granth,* 'Akal Ustat', p.29.
14. Cf. G.S. Talib, *Selections from the Holy Granth,* New Delhi : G.N. Foundation, 1982, pp.185, 173.
15. *Adi Granth,* p.1379.
16. Ibid., p.773.
17. Cf. John Ferguson, *Encyclopaedia of Mysticism,* London : Thames & Hudson, 1976, p.108.
18. N.K.Jain, *Sikh Religion & Philosophy,* New Delhi : Sterling Publishers, 1979, pp. 50-59.
19. Gregory D'Souza, *Transforming Flame,* Mysore : Divya Jyothi Publications, 1988, p.192.
20. Cf. John Ferguson, op.cit., p.168.
21. Ibid., p.108.
22. Ibid., p.28.
23. *Selections,* op.cit., p.196.
24. G.S.Talib (Trans.), *Sri Guru Granth Sahib,* Vol.3, Patiala : P.U., 1987, p.1744.
25. *Selections,* op.cit., p.203.
26. Ibid., p.160.
27. Ibid., pp.160-61.
28. K.L.Seshagiri Rao, 'Guru Nanak & the Hindu Heritage', in *Perspectives,* op. cit.,p.311.
29. 'Guru Nanak to the Guru Granth', ibid., p.522.
30. J.J.Karam, 'Guru Nanak & His Message', ibid., p.318.
31. *Adi-Granth,* p.991.
32. Unesco Series, *The Sacred Writings of the Sikhs,* George Allen & Unwin, 1960 (1965), p.61.
33. *I Am You,* op.cit., p.231.
34. Cf. Wazir Singh, *Philosophy of Sikh Religion,* Delhi : Ess Ess Publications, 1981, p.122.
35. Cf. Wazir Singh, *Humanism of Guru Nanak,* Delhi : Ess Ess Publications, 1977 (quotation from *Love or Perish,* 1956).
36. Sisirkumar Ghose, *Mysticism : Views & Reviews,* New Delhi : Clarion Books, 1987, p.131.
37. Swami Ranganathananda, Kapur Surya Foundation (ed.), *The Human Condition Today,* New Delhi : Clarion Books, 1988, p.86.
38. *I Am You,* op.cit., p.148.
39. Wazir Singh (Trans.) *The Sikh Prayer,* Lucknow, 1982, p.15.
40. Gopal Singh (Trans.) *Thus Spake the Tenth Master,* Patiala :P.U., 1978, p.55.
41. Unesco Series, op.cit., pp.71-72.

42. Ibid., p.135.
43. *Adi-Granth,* p.657.
44. *Adi-Granth,* p.1381.
45. *I Am You,* op. cit., pp.62-3.
46. K.A.Nizami, *The Life & Times of Farid-ud-Din Ganj-i-Shakar, Delhi,* 1955 (1973), pp. 1-2.
47. K. Satchidananda Murty, *Far Eastern Philosophies, Mysore,* 1976, pp.161-2.
48. Satish K.Kapoor, *Cultural Contact & Fusion : Swami Vivekananda in the West,* Jalandhar, 1987, p.47.
49. *I Am You,* op.cit., p.20.
50. *Far Eastern Philosophies,* op.cit., pp.188-91.
51. *Dasam Granth,* 'Akal Ustat' (85).

SIKH PHILOSOPHY AS AKALVADA (NON-TEMPORALISM)

The expression *Akal*, is the sense of Timeless and Immortal, is central and integral to Sikh tradition and thinking.[1] The term is extensively used in the Dasam-Granth hymns, especially by Guru Gobind Singh, who captions one of his poetic compositions *Akal Ustati*, i.e 'In Praise of the Timeless'. However, the concept of Akaal is not peculiar to the Dasam Granth. It was empolyed by Guru Nanak and other Gurus, as well as Bhagat Kabir. Whereas Guru Nanak's use of *Akal* is noted in the Mul-mantra itself, Kabir's reference is found in *Maru-rag* hymns (p. 1104 of G.G.).[2] Guru Ram Das uses the expression a couple of times, in conjunction with *murat* and *purakh* (as in *Sri-rag chhants* and *Gauri-Purabi Karhale*, (pp. 78 and 235 respectively). Guru Arjan refers to *Akal* several times (as for instance, in *Majh*, p.99, *Sorath*, p. 609, *Ramkali*, p.916, *Maru* pp. 1079 and 1082).

It may be noted that the term *Akal* has been used in Gurbani in two forms: (a) as a qualifier or adjective, and (b) as substantive. In the expression Akal Murati, the first part is often treated as a qualifier, even though some interpreters take the two words as independent units, viz. *Akal* and *Murat*, just as Nirbhau and Nirvair are. In the Maru-rag quotations, Kal and Akal have been clearly used as substantives by Guru Arjan and Kabir. The Tenth Guru most often treats the expression as a noun. Akal Ustati is the Praise of Akal and "Hail, O Akal, Hail, O Kirpal!" of Jaap Sahib also takes the related expressions as substantives. The meaning of Akal in this context is 'timeless', 'non temporal', 'deathless', 'not governed by temporal process', or 'not subject to birth, decay and death'. This appears to be negative coining, in each case. But the intent is affirmative. Akal as deathless or non-temporal implies everlasting reality, eternal Being, or transcendent Spirit; it further implies Eternity, Being, or Essence. The linguistic form may be negative, but the semantic implication is unmistakably affirmative.

The author of Jaap Sahib[3] in the Dasam Granth has depicted the Supreme Reality as Akal with its innumerable manifestations. It is the same Reality that was given the epithet of Sat/i in the Guru Granth Sahib. 'Sat/i' is the primordial name of the eternal Being (Maru, p 1083). All the names that we utter in respect of God are functional or attributive names. The basic reality is nameless. Guru Gobind Singh expressly calls it ANAME (nameless). But, even namelessness can serve as a name.

When we say Brahaman is featureless, 'featurelessness' becomes its feature. In order to give expression to our sense of the Beyond, that which defies all expression or description, we coin several terms, just as Nothingness, Emptiness, Big Zero, Sunya, as well as Formless, Nir-akar, Nirankar and Nirgun. But again, Nirankar is a name, and so are other epithets so coined. Perhaps, we cannot do without names. It is our linguisic compulsion to assign a name or symbol to anything we know. It is human compulsion. This explains our propensity to coin a name for the Nameless. Sikhism has chosen Sat/i and Akal, in order to signify what it regards as the Eternal Spirit, beyond the pale of time, temporality or cosmic processes.

Time and Eternity in Sikhism

Guru Gobind Singh's Bani is a repository of concepts and terms, especially of the epithets relating to 'time'. Besides Kal and Akal he uses Maha Kal (macro-time) and Sarb-Kal (all time) to indicate a Being above and beyond the eventful time of the universe. For him, Kal itself is a dimension of Akal, the only difference being the process that characterizes temporal events, and the eternality of Akal. Every occurrence or event has beginning and end, each event is a link in the on-going process of Time. The cosmic drama or the wondrous show of the world is all a creation of Time. The power of Time controls the worldly events; the only entity independent of time is Time itself, and that is Akal, the Timeless. That is why God is both Time and Timeless in Guru Gobind Singh's Bani. The aspect of Time is the immanent aspect, the presence of Spiritual Essence in each worldly occurrence. It is the 'personality' of the Supreme, the *chit* or consciousness of Sat-Chit-Anand.[4] The other, transcendent aspect, is the Eternal, the Beyond, the Inexpressible, the Fathomless, Nirgun Brahman, assigned the name Akal.

The doctrine of Timeless Being runs parallel to the Advaitic philosophy of Shankara. The latter holds the ultimate reality as *advaita* (non-dual), which is of the nature of Brahman Atman, that is pure consciousness. The soul is not different from Brahman; the world is an illusory appearance. When enlightenment dawns, the individual self and Maya are no more; the Brahman as sole reality remains. In other words, the duality of 'I' and 'Brahman', of illusion and reality, is eliminated. The term 'non-dual' or *advaita* is negative coinage that, like Akal, is affirmative in its meaning. The doctrine of Advaitavada, in its linguistic form, appears to be negative yet it points to oneness of the ulitimate reality, bearing monistic implications. If further stretched, it turns out to be absolutism, leaving no scope for any autonomous unit or entity, other than the Absolute. Thus, Non-dualism is the title of the Vedantic theory of Shankara, and distinguishes it from all the other philosophical theories, e.g. Dualism, Realism, Sunyavada, Existentialism, Evolutionism, etc. The title derives from Shankara's conception of the highest reality, the central theme of his philosophy. On this analogy, Sikh philosophy may rightly be designated Akalvada (non-temporalism).

The Akal of Sikhism is not a fixed, unmoving substance, but the spiritual principle of the entire cosmic existence. The phenomenal world emanates from Spirit, and the Spirit permeates the world. Like a tree with flourishing branches, the absolute Spirit moves with the motions of the worldly objects and energizes them. According to Gurbani, the Formless Being keeps on creating the phenomenal world. He creates and recreates and carries on with his creative activity. Akal of the Sikh conception is not consciousness pure and simple, blank and void, but is Creative Spirit, as the expression 'Karta Purakh' implies. In other words, creativity is the core of Akal. And it is creativity that shows up in the dimension of Kal. Acting through Time, the Timeless creates beings of the world. It does not seem possible to conceive of creativity without conceiving temporality or time. It is through creativity that the Timeless transforms itself from Nirgun to Sargun, from *aphur* state into *saphur* state, from the pre-creation essence into cosmic existence.

The creativity of Akal is not confined to the timeless and temporal aspects of the Supreme. Through its Sargun facet the Nirgun assumes the character of the Divine, of the good gracious God, the loving Lord or Prabhu of the devotees. From 'It' the Ultimate becomes 'He' - the person with whom communication is sought and established. From 'Akal', He becomes 'Sri-Akal'. The Sikh slogan and popular form of greeting 'Sat/i Sri Akal' succintly conveys the idea of Timeless Being that is the singular Eternal Reality. The pharase combines the concepts of Satya and Akal, implying that the Eternal and the Timeless are one: Satya itself is the Everlasting Lord. Thus, the creative essence turns the metaphysical Being into active principle of the world, into conscious Power involved in the cosmic process, into Hero of the world, cherishing his creation with delight. Being the beneficent Lord, he lends some of his creativity to the created beings. Humanity draws its creativity and creative energy from the Divine reservoir of Creativity.

The Sikh tradition is imbued with heroism and valour that are inspired by the conceptual framework of Akalvada. The Akal of Guru Gobind Singh is All Steel (Sarb-Loh), a symbolic expression for the valiant heroes of his conception. Guru Nanak had applied the epithet of Jodha-Mahabali – Surma[5] to the valiant in the human as well as divine form. In depicting the Akal, the Tenth Guru associated the attributes of *Sarb-Kal, Sarb Dyal, Sarb Pal* with his creativity. He calls him Glorious and great, Super form, Yogi of yogis, Moon of moons, Melody of music, Rhythm of the dance, liquidity of waters, movement of the winds.[6] He is Akal as well as Kirpal, the compassionate Lord. In fact, the whole composition of Jaap Sahib, with its wide range of attributive names, presents the twin framework of Akal-Kripal, like the female-male image of *ardhanarishvara.*[7] The Impersonal appears through all persons, the Timeless encompasses all the temporal beings emanating from his Essence. He transcends the human world, yet is He the compassionate. His timeless essence permeates the temporal existence.

The concept of Akal, cnetral to Jaap Sahib, has percolated to the social, political and cultural life of the Sikh community. Inspired by its theme, they call the Gurus' Bani 'Akali Bani.' The political wing of the community is known as Akali Dal. The slogan 'Sat/i Sri Akal' has become a form of greetings for the Punjabis in general. The process had been initiated much earlier, half a century before the advent of Guru Gobind Singh on the scene. The Sixth Guru had already identified the throne built at Amritsar as 'Akal Takht' - the Throne of the Timeless Being.

Akal Murat/i and Akal Purakh

The pair of elements *Akal* (non temporal) and *murat/i* (image), occurring in the Mul Mantra[8] itself, lierally implies 'timeless image'. Elsewhere, in the compositions of Guru Ram Das (GG p. 78), and Guru Arjan Dev (pp. 99, 609, 916 and 1082), the expression Akal Murat/i reinforces the original meaning of Divine Reality that is beyond the process of time, and yet permeates the cosmic forms. The non-temporal Being transcends the space-time framework and, as such, is Formless. However, in its manifest aspect, the same Being assumes the cosmic form. The Sikh vision of God combines the Formless and its expression in natural forms, the transcendent and the immanent, the Essence (Spirit) and Existence (creation).

The expresion 'Akal Murat/i' lends itself to interpretation in two ways. The exegetes who treat it as one term, take *akal* in the adjectival form that qualifies the substantive Murat/i, the whole expression implying Everlasting Form equivalent to the Supreme Being. Those approaching the pair *akal* and *murat/i* analytically, treat both the units independently, each expressing an attribute of the Divine Reality, believed to transcend time and space, yet manifest in space-time forms. But, despite the divergence of approach, both interpretations agree in substance, namely, the featureless eternal Reality assumes features and modes of empirical existence. To put it differently, 'Akal Murat/i' presents a synthesis of Nirgun and Sargun facets of the Absolute-God of Guru Nanak's vision.

The term Akalpurakh stands for the Divine Being or simply God. Like Akal Murat/i, it is composed of two units, viz. *akal* (non-temporal) and *purakh* (person). The latter finds place in the Mul Mantra[8] in conjunction with Karta (Creator), the whole expression implying the Creator Divine Person. The Sikh tradition has adopted the expression Akalpurakh as a household term, used in common parlance just like its equivalents, such as Vaheguru and Satinam.[9]

'Purakh' as a linguistic symbol derives from the Sanskrit *Prurusha* (Man), invariably employed in the masculine gender. In the Vedic literature, the term also stands for the world, indicating the entirety of universal existence. In the Indian systems of Sankhya and Yoga, Purusha, as one of the two cardinal metaphysical principles, stands for spirituality or simply consciousness, which exerts influence on *Prakriti* (nature) that is physical in its make-up. The core of *purusha,* therefore, is conscious-ness, denoted by *chit* in the Sat-Chit-Anand conception of the Absolute. This connotation of the term invests 'Purakh' with spirituality or self, rendering it as the Divine Person. Combined with *akal,* the expression as a whole means the Everlasting Divine Person (God), in the Sikh tradition and literature.

'Akalpurakh' as such is rarely used in the Guru-Granth compositions. We come across the term in Guru Ram Das' Gauri Purabi Karhale (p. 235) in the inverse form, viz. Purakh Akal/i. However, the Dasam Granth compositions employ *Akalpurakh* as a substitute for God, the Eternal Being, transmitting the expression for use by posterity. Akal being a cardinal and central concept of Sikhism, its use alongside *Purakh* accords a distinct theological status to *Akalpurakh* thereby ensuring its popular appeal among Sikh circles.

NOTES

1. Cf. G.S.Talib, *Selections from the Holy Granth*, New Delhi : G.N.Foundation, 1982.
2. Guru Granth Sahib, the Holy Book of the Sikhs, compiled in 1604, consists of 1430 pages in print. (The scripture is indicated as G.G. in the text; the pp. refer to its folios.)
3. Jaap Sahib is the first composition in the Dasam Granth (The holy book of the Tenth Guru) accorded a place of reverence next only to the Guru Granth, by the Sikh community.
4. Sat-Chit-Anand (lit. Being-Consciousness-Bliss) is the traditional Indian epithet for the Absolute-cum-God; it stands for Brahman, the Supreme Reality of Indian vision.,
5. 'Jodha-Mahabali-Surma' is a favourite expression of Guru Nanak, indicating heroic qualities of a valiant-courageous crusader, championing righteous causes.
6. Cf. Gopal Singh's rendering of Jaap Sahib, in *Thus Spake the Tenth Master*, Patiala : Punjabi University, 1978.
7. 'Ardhanarishvara' (lit. half female, half male) stands for the Indian image of Lord Shiva whose one-half represents his consort, implying the male-female nature of the divine principle.
8. 'Mul-mantra' is the popular name applied to the basic credal formula with which the holy Guru Granth opens. It signifies the monotheistic intent of the entire text that follows.
9. Both 'Waheguru' and 'Sat/i Nam' stand for God in Sikh parlance. The former expresses the human sense of wonder for the Wonderful Enlightener, whereas the latter is indicitive of the primordial, everlasting Reality Supreme.

THE DIVINE ORDINANCE IN SIKHISM
(A perspective on Hukam)

The conceptual framework of Sikhism incorporates two sets of concepts; the foundational and the superstructural. *Hukam*, being a cardinal principle of Sikh thought, belongs to the first set. It is one of the essential, indispensable constituents of Sikh metaphysics and cosmology, as well as fundamental article of faith. Its importance may be gauged from the fact that the term *Hukam* occurs in the very first stanza of the *Japuji,* the opening text of the Sikh scirpture, and the entire second stanza revolves round the concept *Hukam.* In the conceptual hierarchy of Sikh philosophy, *Hukam* occupies a place next to *Akal* and *Karta* (the eternal/formless Being and the Creator Person or spiritual source of all existence). What is established by the creative principle (the Divine) is the cosmic order, that is, manifest aspect of the Unmanifest, and that embodies *Hukam,* according to the Sikh View.

One of the key-concepts of Sikhism, *Hukam* as a linguistic symbol has its roots in the Islamic/Sufistic thought originally expressed in the Arabic. There it means simply a command issuing forth from authority, its equivalent in Persian being *Firman* (order) addressed by someone superior or person in command to a person or a group junior in rank. The connotation of *Hukam* in Punjabi, while retaining the Arabic-Persian colouring of order and commandment, widens the semantic range to cover 'will', particularly the Divine Will; sequence, system or law in the sense of Divine Ordinance; recognition and acceptance of Divine Power transcending human energies. One peculiar usage of *Hukam* in Punjabi, is the relational form of the term viz. *Hukami,* in the sense of the authority, which in *Gurbani* is the Godhead, from whom the order or the ordinance issues. (The adverbial form *Hukami/n* meaning 'by or through the will of God' is not to be confused with the relative term *Hukami.*)

Two characteristics of *Hukam*, shared by Islamic and Sikh theologies are the inevitability and mystery of the Divine Will. As put by Professor G.S.Talib, "*Hukam* in Islamic theology stands for 'commandment', 'the code' etc., and not for the mystical 'ordinance' which is what it means in Sikh thought." But whether it is the code or the Ordinance, the Divine Will stands for a fixed law that admits no deviation. Again, there is no answer to the mystery of Hukam. To quote Talib again : " Philosophically *Hukam* is the apprehension of that mystery which underlines all existence, and which can express itself only in the action of submission and resignation. It is the realization by the particle of its finitude against the infinitude of the Divine...It is the idealist's vision which sees a Divine Purpose in everything, and finding the understanding of the mystery beyond the power of man, puts itself in the attitude of wonder and acceptance.'' The inscrutable, relentless, immutable law of God is the implication that underlies *Hukam* in the Islamic and, to a large extent, Sikh thought.

The genesis of Hukam in the classical Indian thought is encountered in the figures of *Rit*(Rta) and *Vrat*. The former stands for the cosmic order. ''Rta is an intelligent principle that regulates the cosmos as well as the individual.'' If Rit pervades the entire cosmic existence, *Vrat* is the principle of functioning in all the sub-systems forming part of the cosmos. Both the Vedic terms are precursors of *dharma*, a widely employed concept with a variety of meanings that include 'law of nature', the principle holding the celestial bodies in controlled motion, the power holding the earth in balance, besides righteousness, duty and faith. *Hukam* is not far from *dharma* in its wider connotation of the law governing the macrocosm as well as the microcosm. In the *Dharm Khand* realm (occurring in the *Japuji*) reference is made to the law of Dharma operating in 'the starry heavens above' and to its analogue, the law of Karma, 'within', that is, the human world.

Apart from Dharma the concept of *Hukam* has parallels in the various branches of thought, in science and naturalistic metaphysics, in theistic and non-theistic philosophies. The Marxian idea of Necessity comes close to *Hukam*, both pointing to the non-human realm of inexorable law governing matter, life and their evolutes. In relation to man, Necessity of Marxian conception turns from blind necessity into something knowable. Man frees himself from the rigours of Necessity in the degree he knows and comprehends that necessity. The well-known saying of F.Engels, viz. 'Freedom is the recognition of Necessity', shorn of its ideological connotation, appears to be a replica of Guru Nanak's verse :

> He who recognizes the ordinance, Nanak,
> Never shall assert his ego again. (*Japuji,* stanza II)

Interestingly enough, both the authorities cited have firm belief in the knowability of the laws of nature as also in the liberating influence of such knowledge. The most incomprehensible thing about the world is that it is comprehensible, that is, to the human mind; and the greatest shackle of man is his own ego from which emancipation is sought through comprehension of the Divine ordinance, that is *Hukam*.

Facticity is another concept, thrown up by existentialist thinkers, notably Heidegger and Sartre, that is in close proximity of *Hukam.* Man finds himself in a particular situation which is not his choosing; he is simply 'thrown' into the situation. Moreover, he finds a set of facts about himself which defines his situation. Existentialism understands facticity in relation to the past of the individual which can never change. The antecedents making up what he is, are like God-given facts, but, insist the existentialists, man is free to determine his future essence. He is the author of his own values. The implication of this insistence is that it is only through human consciousness that values come into the world, even though values are to be found in the world. The teaching of *Gurbani* upholds the view that it is given to man to make or unmake himself, to move in the direction of being 'regenerate' or 'degenerate' an individual. Without seeking to change the facts of his past, man is free to transcend his facticity.

Some other interpretations of *Hukam* may be given in terms of destiny and determinism; fear and discipline; cosmic energy and supernatural power. One may even use the expression 'fatalism' to describe *Hukam,* though such an extremist reading of the concept is hardly warranted by the textual references. The generally acceptable construction placed on the concept in Sikh circles equates *Hukam* with Divine Volition. "The entire creation depends on *Hukam* i.e. God's Will," says Professor Harbans Singh. This *Hukam* is the principle of all life. This creation is the outcome of the Will of the conscious Being. "Hukam is the fundamental principle of God's activity; thus it is the principle of all activity."

Hukam as the cosmic discipline ordained by the Divine accords with its meaning as the principle of activity. The term *bhaya/bhai* (lit.fear) is employed in the text to denote discipline maintained by the celestial bodies. In fear is the sun, in fear the moon, says Guru Nanak. Billions of miles they traverse endlessly without halt. According to the Guru, the entire universe obeys the Will; nothing is outside the pale of *Hukam.* The discipline is equally applicable to man. In fact, the category of 'fear' more appropriately belongs to the human sphere. Man is exhorted to live in 'fear' of God, shedding all other fears. Within the limits of his over-all destiny, man is given the choice and freedom to lead life fearlessly, at the same time inculcating fear of an exalted kind. Fear or discipline maintained by the suns and stars, in the physical universe, is at the level of blind necessity; the type of fear prescribed for man is of a higher order, of the order of consciousness and freedom.

Contemporary thinking in the circle of science has veered around the concept of Energy, in order to explain the multiplicity of phenomena in the universe as also the forms of material objects. There is no matter; it is all energy. The material particle (atom) of the nineteenth century has given place to the sub-atomic packets of energy; the sun and stars are nothing but formations of energy; the electro-magnetic waves, light-rays, photons, *elan-vital*,- all are energy. The metaphyical implication of the concept consists in the reconstruction of reality in terms of one single source of the phenomenal world, viz. Energy. If energy is conceived in physical terms, the universe may be viewed as materialistic; but if energy is another name of 'power' and is conceived as endowed with 'consciousness', philosophical idealism is the result. The *chit* in the *Sat-Chit-Anand* syndrome refers to the dimension of consciousness in the Absolute. The primal, conscious power, in other words the Spirit, is at the base of all cosmic phenomena; and this Spirit is precisely the sole source of *Hukam* or the Divine Ordinance.

The Divine and the Will of the Divine are often taken as two entities. Nationally this separation of the two sounds correct, and a distinction between the *Hukami* and *Hukam* may well be maintained. Yet, experientially, the Ordainer and the Ordinance, in the case of God, seem fused into one. The Divine Being installs himself as the cosmic order; the Creator is immanent in his creation. The Ordainer *(Hukami)* is not distinct from his Ordinance *(Hukam)*. From the concealed, unmanifest state, He springs into the revealed, manifest state. The epithets of *gupat* and *paragt* are employed in *Gurbani* for the two states, which correspond to the pre-creation state of the Void and cosmic state, respectively. In the *Maru Solhe* composition, Guru Nanak speaks of the inexpressible darkness that prevailed in the primoridal state of the Absolute. He talks in terms of the 'trance' of the Formless Spirit, its power, its creativity and potentiality for self-manifestation. There were no contours of the universe, no suns, no stars, no earth. But, "as and when He willed/He brought the world into being/and vaulted heavens without support." "Establishing continents, worlds and underworlds /from the state of void unreavealed/Self-manifest became He."

What is the principle of the working of cosmic existence, according to the Gurus? Philosophers have ascribed humanly contrived principles of love and strife, attraction and repulsion, unity and differentiation, integration and disintegration, in their attempts to explain the dialectics of creation. In the fifth century B.C., the Greek Philosopher Empedocles presented the hypothesis of Love-Hate forces acting in the world of nature. *Udkarakh* and *akarkh* (expansion and contraction) as cosmological principles have been suggested by thinkers in India and elsewhere. Guru Nanak and his successors employ the terminology of *sanjog* and *vijog* in order to convey their view of the ultimate principles governing the entire creation: "unification and alienation drive affairs of the world." Such principles emanate from the *Hukam* of the Creator-Ordainer.

The concept of *Hukam*, in the sense of Divine Ordinance pervading the cosmic existence, is also found in conjunction with the concept *Reza or Bhana* in Sikhism. The term *reza*, of Arabic origin, with Sufistic hue, expresses like *Hukam* a cardinal principle of Sikh faith. Its equivalent in Punjabi, viz *bhana*, has percolated to the popular level in the Punjabi culture. *Bhana* is what appeals to God; it is Divine pleasure, His sweet will. In this sense, *Hukam, Reza and Bhana* come closest to one another. However, *Hukam* in its purely metaphysical connotation is a non-human, pre-cosmic, as well as cosmic principle, whereas *reza* and *bhana* have to be interpreted in relation to man. *Reza* implies resigning oneself to the will of God, so does *bhana*. Both suggest whole-hearted approval and acceptance of what is ordained for man by the Master.

Besides *Hukam* and Reza/Bhana, another dimension of the governing principle of Nature, according to the Sikh teaching, is Divine Grace. Between the Creator and his creation, Grace forms the nexus, leading to the pure legality of *Hukam* an element of patriarchal consideration and affection. Grace is interpreted in Sikhism as the Divine response to filial sentiments of living beings. It is the cosmic interest in human affairs. Without grace, the Divine Ordinance would be a rigid, inflexible law, devoid of all 'care' for the creatures. The Sikh view of cosmology presents the picture of a loving, caring, human law-giver. This is the outcome of *Hukam*-cum-Grace approach of the mentors of the Sikh faith.

God in Sikhism is occasionally posed as really a hard nut to crack. He is not pleased by any sort of mannerism, formal ceremonies, offerings, recitations etc. He cannot be forced, cajoled, or persuaded to alter his designs and course of activities. No power on earth can claim to have authority or control over Him. Only his loving devotees, the bhaktas, are able to influence Him; and they are the recipients of special graces bestowed by the Lord. The Divine-Devotee relationship being inscrutable, and the Hukam-Grace principle being of a mysterious nature, the exact mechanism of the functioning of *Hukam* and Grace defies fulsome expression. Guru Nanak, in the opening couplet of the *Japuji's* second stanza, states: "Through his Will emerge all forms/the Will a mystery remains." Loving devotion and resigning oneself to the Will divine serves as the key to unlock the mysterious mansion of the Creator-Ordainer-Gracious Being.

Though drawn from the Semitic sources, the concept of *Hukam* in Sikhism has worked itself as functionally independent of its origins. The Sikh view of *Hukam*, with greater stress on its metaphysical intent, as also on its liberating role in terms of the workability of *Hukam*, nevertheless retains the simple meaning of 'God's commandment' at the popular level. Here it has greater affinity with the Semitic import of the concept. For the common man, the world came into existence as ordered by God; nothing happens in the world without God's Will; death too obeys the Divine command whose majesty cannot be challenged. The only course open to man is to abide by the Divine Will, for defiance is of no avail. It is His will that will prevail. Then why not resign oneself to that Will?

The Sikh way of life combines stress on *Hukam* with an activist approach to problems of life. Resignation to God's volition is interpreted neither in terms of fatalism nor of escapism. The disciple of the Gurus is supposed to lead his/her life in accordance with the spiritual discipline and moral code prescribed in the scripture and handed down by tradition. One's effort is directed towards personal salvation as well as fulfilment of the collective well-being. In other words, one is to perform one's duty in society, guided by the values indicated in *Gurbani*. This is one part of the prescription. The other part is surrender of oneself to the Divine dispensation, so far as the outcome of one's effort is concerned. Herein lies the precept of *Hukam-Reza*, that is abiding by the sweet will of God in all situation of life.

A PERSPECTIVE ON DIVINE WILL

One of the key-concepts in the gamut of Sikh thought, the Arabic *reza*, with its nearmost Punjabi equivalent, *bhana*, has stood the test of time as the bedrock of Sikh faith unfolded by tradition. The Gurus as well as the Sikhs as a community, have firmly adhered to *reza-bhana* as their fundamental article of faith. As put by G.S. Talib, "*Reza*, like *Hukam*, is also Divine will and these two terms are generally employed in the Guru's teaching in conjunction." "The basic idea implicit in *Hukam* and *Reza* is the imperative nature, the supremacy of the Divine Will and the duty of man to submit to such Will, whether joy comes to him or sorrow."

The lexical meaning of *Reza* points to approval or liking, be pleased with, have appeal to; it also conveys the sense of 'to be content', 'pleased to choose'; pleasant, agreeable, acceptable; as also 'one who is content' or 'well pleased'. The *Kashrulmahjub* of Syyad Hajveri explicates *reza* in the context of various schools of Sufi thought. The two-fold meaning of the term that stands out in its elaboration is, first, God being pleased with man, and second, man content with God's will. Reza as employed in Sikh thought subscribes primarily to its meaning as the Divine Will itself, though taking equal cognizance of the other meaning, viz. the attitude of submission on man's part to the Will divine.

The opening stanza of Guru Nanak's Japuji refers to Reza, in conjunction with Hukam, as though laying down direction for the way of life for all who care, commending to man the path of resignation, which otherwise too is pre-ordained and igrained in his being. The Guru never tires of asserting this faith in his compositons. He avers - "The blessings are in the hands of the Lord; none can force Him to part with any of these." - He bestows his grace on whomsoever He pleases. The inscrutable Divine Will is at the base of the entire cosmic existence. It was His *bhana,* his 'sweet will' so to speak, which was instrumental in the world's coming into being: from the concealed, unmanifest state of inexpressible Void, became He manifest through the order of Nature. Both 'good' and 'evil' in the world are divinely ordained. "And what of those condemned to pain and miseries ever? Such blessing in disguise the Bounteous One may shower." - (Japuji)

The Divine Will, in the sense of inexorable ordinance or law of nature, is intimately related to the problem of determinism versus free will. As presented in the seventeenth-century terminology, "the cornerstone of Newtonian mechanics was the Principle of Universal Causality : every occurrence can be established in a law like connection with some sufficient set of antecedent causes." Accordingly, "every human action is presumed to be determined completely by antecedent events." Not that science and philosophy in the twentieth century abandoned the deterministic hypothesis and opted for freedom both in the physical and human spheres. The emphases changed, new perspectives emerged, the relationship between determinism and indeterminism was reviewed in depth, the two converging to each other. Seen in the new light, human actions are not caused by external factors alone; some at least are determined by the person concerned.

Existentialist philosophers, in particular, have brought the question of freedom into focus. The Sartrean approach, for instance, is couched in these words : "Man, as finite freedom, is free within the contingencies of his finitude." "We are absolutely free to form the project and try to climb; we are not absolutely free to reach the top of the rock." To be both 'complete'(i.e. determined) and 'free', is regarded as "man's impossible ideal," since man is "condemned" to be free, economic determinism of Marx notwithstanding. Blessing or curse, a measure of freedom for man has to be recognized, if only to provide justification for ethics and spirituality. The voluminous Holy Book of the Sikhs keeps on reminding man to make the choice : to become regenerate a person, rather than degenerate.

The freedom to transcend one's tragic situation, characterized by suffering *(a la* Buddha and Farid), or by anguish (as per Sartre), or by anxiety (as per Paul Tillich), entails effort on one's part. Rare would be a moral philosopher or spiritual leader exhorting men to reject effort or activity in realizing their summun bonum. Sikhism prides itself in subscribing to an avtivist philosophy of life. If a passive resignation to the will of God were the teaching, it would not possibly reconcile with the activist model. Perhaps one needs to read deeper meaning in the message. Let one act within the framework of one's finite being, choosing the set of values suited to one's deliverance, and surrender oneself to the Ordainer's Reza as regards the outcome.

Sikhism rejects the ideology that advocates *khudi* or sense of individuation, repugnant to the teaching of *reza/bhana.* The ego is to be contained, not to be boosted up or asserted. "When *khudi* is no more, joy descends : mind and body regain health," says Guru Arjan. Egoism is not only a malady, not only a shackle, it is negation of faith in divinity, and contradiction of the spirit of resignation. Even though not a philosophy of protest, Sikhism allows freedom to raise voice of protest, as Guru Nanak did : "People suffered endless tortures, and wailed, didst Thou have no compassion for them?" Yet, this protest is indicative of abiding faith in God who loves and cares. The boon a Sikh seeks for oneself is the spirit of ascendance, the high morale resulting from faith; his prayer is for the well-being of entire humanity in the will of God.

The spirit of resigning oneself to the divine will is obverse of the faith in the goodness of God. It is one thing to say that what He wills, will prevail, it is another to recognize in the depths of one's soul that what He wills and does, is all to the good of mankind, nay, of life itself. The apparent suffering in the world, injustice, depravity, vice, in a word, all that is known as evil, dissolves in the unalterable faith in the Divine Good. Faith has been defined as man's participation in God's dealings with humankind. For, the locus of faith is persons; faith is insight into and response of human beings to the truth and goodness that is Divine. The faith inculcated by the spirit of *reza* demands, in addition, suspension, perhaps relinquishment, of human judgement that pronounces on good and evil. The Divine is the Judge, not man. The profundity of such faith illustrates itself in the martyrdom of a Socrates and Mansur, the Christ and Guru Arjan, Guru Tegh Bahadur and his juvenile grandsons.

The Sikh history, in its short span of five centuries, bears testimony to the spirit of willing submission, of *Reza*, of *Bhana*, in the face of heavy odds. The eighteenth century's holocausts, the extreme tortures leading to death of the young and old, women and children, convincingly speak of the unfolding of spiritual inspiration that was *Reza*. This was the most potent force shaping the Sikh tradition. The spirit of *Reza* in this case is not the same as acquiescence, or abject submission, in a situation of no escape. Perception of inevitability may produce cowardice, or it may invoke the response of valiant welcome to Divine dispensation, if the conditioning has been of *Bhana* - "What pleases Thee, is sweet to me."

Ultimately, it is a question of the recognition of mystery involved in the cosmic affairs. The man of Reza knows that what he knows of the starry heavens and earth, of life and mind, is only partial, limited and finite. Above all is the mystery of the Divine itself, which to the human mind is not fully revealed, unless one is blessed with the insight and vision of a *Brahman-giani*, for:

> As high as He, one has to be,
> Only to realize, how high is He.
>
> -(Japuji)

The teaching of Gurbani awakens one to the 'opportunity' of human life gifted to him/her, to the mystery of grace that may descend upon one, to the inculcation of the spirit of *Reza* and the belief that liberation from the bondage will be obtained through His *Bhana*, for this much is certain; beyond this no claim is to be made.

THE SIKH VIEW OF COSMIC ORDER

The Sikh cosmology is an extension of the metaphysics of Sikhism and its doctrine of the Godhead. The Supreme Being of the Sikh view is the Creator-Person, who manifests himself through the process of cosmic creation. One essential feature of the cosmological speculation involved is belief in the pre-creation state of the Absolute. Religious cosmologies, adventurous as they are, tread upon regions beyond the pale of scientific investigation. Human fancy and creative imagination do play a significant part in the theories of creation and the creator found in the sacred books of the East and the West. Poetic intuitions of the prophets and religious leaders offer insights which, though not subject to verification, leave a powerful impress on the human mind. It is amazing how close affinity some of the cosmological beliefs of the Sikhs have with the Vedic as well as Semitic ventures in the field. Some features of the Sikh view of cosmic creation compare favourably with the cosmological models put forward by modern science. The age-old expression Brahmand (Brahman+und) literally means "cosmic egg" - an epithet that contemporary astronomy has thrown up to depict the embryonic state of the universe.

Cosmological Formulations in Gurbani

Sikhism presents the intuitive insights of its mentors into reality and its modes, through the medium of poetry. While building up its doctrinal edifice largely on the conceptual foundations provided by India's philosophical heritage, Sikhism rejected the mythical and patently superstitious elements clouding the traditional thinking. In its cosmology, Sikhism tried to do without the tales of a giant dismembered by gods, or the mating of a god-goddess pair. Guru Nanak treats such features of the tradition as figments of imagination. In contrast with the faith in "three deities" carrying on the roles of creation, preservation and annihilation, Guru Nanak puts forth his thesis that it is all Divine Will: God himself ordains the worldly ways and performs all the roles.[1]

The depiction of Guru Nanak's pre-cosmic state of the Absolute is remarkably similar to Rigvedic creation-hymn. He talks in terms of the 'trance' of the Formless Spirit, the Absolute Void, the 'power' of Being, its creativity, and potentiality for manifestion and self-revelation. In his *Maru Solhe* composition, he says:

> In the beginning was inexpressible darkness;
> Neither the earth nor sky there was,

The Infinite Will alone prevailed,
Neither day and night, nor the moon and sun did exist,
The Absolute Void was in eternal stance.
No source of creation, no speech,
No air, no water there were;
No production, no consumption, no arrival, no departure,
No lands or nether regions, not the seven seas,
Nor waters flowing down streams...
As and when He willed, He brought the world into being
And vaulted heavens without support.
Created He Brahma, Vishnu, Shiva
And instilled in earthly beings
Sense of attachment over-bearing...
Establishing continents, worlds and underworlds,
From state of void unrevealed, Self-manifest became He.[2]

Guru Angad adds a note of Divine immanence in his cosmological formulation, in one of his verses:

This world is the Abode of the holy Lord,
The holy One abides in the world.[3]

In order to poetically depict the immeasurably long duration of the Absolute Spirit's self-absorption, expressions like innumerable eras of nebulous darkness, and thirty-six ages of divine 'trance' have been used by Guru Nanak and Guru Amar Das. "God makes and remakes the world." - "Like a skilful player, He performs the feat (of creation)." Elsewhere too, references to the repeated cycles of creation and dissolution are found. A major conclusion that emerges is in regard to the concept of continual creation at the hands of God. As put by Fred Hoyle : "of all the various possibilities that have been suggested, continuous creation is easily the most satisfactory."[4]

Guru Nanak's depiction of the immensity and vastness of the created universe, is realistic enough:

Millions are the underworlds, millions float in space:
Despairing of the final count, Vedas give up stake.[5]

According to the Guru, "the Lord is engaged in the endless process of creation." Guru Arjan refers to the "reality" of the world on the plea that the creation emanating from the Divine cannot be false or unreal:

Real Himself, real is all He makes;
The whole creation from the Divine emanates;
If He so wills, expansion initiates;
If He so wills, all in one concentrates.[6]

Dialectics of Creation

Philosophers have ascribed humanly contrived principles of love and strife, attraction and repulsion, unity and differentiation, integration and disintegration, in their attempts to explain the working of cosmic existence. Guru Nanak and his successors employ the terminology of *Sanjog* and *Vijog*, in order to convey their view of the ultimate principles governing the entire creation. "Unification and alienation drive affairs of the world," says Guru Nanak in the Japuji.[7] Guru Amar Das, in similar vein, avers: "God created the modes of Union and Seperation, thus laying the foundation of all existence." In the fifth century B.C., the Greek philosopher Empedocles presented the hypothesis of Love-Hate forces acting in the world of nature. His view is not dissimilar to its Indian counterpart, viz. *Sanjog-Vijog* pair. The poet of *Benati Chaupai* talks in terms of expansion and contraction (*udkarkh* and *akarkh*), as parallel cosmological principles:

> When the Creator projects himself
> The world and creatures all take shape:
> When He draws in and attracts
> All embodiments relapse into Him.[8]

Perhaps the same principle is at the base of the modern Pulsating Universe (or the Oscillating Universe) theory, according to which the universe compresses and expands in alternating phases.

The whole intent of Gurbani is to accept the spiritual Essence as the origin and source of all existence. The pure 'essence' without an embodiment in its blissful freedom, takes on the grab of 'existence'. The Spirit is one, it is unity, though not a blank unity or pure void. From the one (that is unmanifest aspect) it turns into the plural (manifest aspect). Again, from the infinity of forms, it returns to its original singularity. Pluralism inherent in the philosophy of existence, turns into monism that characterizes the metaphysics of essence. This is yet another dimension of the dialectics of creation in Sikhism.

The Supreme Being is depicted in Gurbani, not only as the author of creation, but also as the ordainer of the world. Sometimes, the universe is belived to be an emanation from the individuating ego in man, but this interpretation of the Gurus' compositions scarcely accords with the general intent of the Bani. Granted that the 'existence' of the world cannot be dissociated from 'experience'. Yet, this relation does not entail dependence of existence on experience. How does the world *appear*? It apperas in the consciousness of living beings. But who is the author of the world? Not human ego; it is the Supreme itself. Accordingly, the governing principle of nature is the Ordinance of the Divine, the *hukam*, that maintains the elements, the land and waters, the stars and planets, in fact the entire spatio-temporal cosmos and its processes. All matter, life and mind obey the discipline of that single absolute authority which transcends all dicipline, control or command. All else is under the 'fear' of the One that is fearless in Himself.

The Status of Maya

Maya as a philosophic category commands awe and respect in the Indian tradition. The Advaitic conception of maya is designed to serve as the fundamental mode of existence endowed with unique and matchless powers. Its being is conceived as paralle to that of Brahman, for both are treated as beginningless (*anadi*) and beyond adequate expression in human terms. The world of names and forms is a product of *maya*, which is indicative of its powers of creation and of concealing reality. Only to a spiritually advanced individual *maya* ceases to be, and Brahman alone remains . By implication, *maya* continues to exist for the rest of mankind, as an objective entity. It is this extreme objectification of *maya* in the Vedantic theory, to which Sikhism does not subscribe. The Gurus do not assign to it the character of a mataphysical category, in the framework of their scriptural compositions.

Of course, the figures of Brahma, Vishnu and Shiva, as also of maya frequently find place in the *Bani*, indicative of the link with the tradition of Indian thought. But these figures stand for the powers of the Divine in the *Gurbani* diction. Brahma cannot be taken in the literal sense of a creator with absolute authority. Likewise, maya as an independent creative power would be out of place with the spirit of Nanak-Bani. The only agency that governs the process of nature is nature itself as an embodiment of the Divine Ordinance. If this aspect of nature were to be identified as *maya*, no contradiction would be involved, since the existence of nature is recognized in the *Bani* in the form of *qudrat* of the *Qadir*. However, if nature is viewed as an independent realm, final in itself, then the interpretation fails to cohere with Guru Nanak's over-all view of reality. He himself describes such a world as false - that is, a world which is falsely viewed as real in itself, without the presence of its creative Spirit. The thrust of the poetic depiction seems to be that the world is real if the Divine immanence is realized in every part and corner of it; the same world is false and unreal if we fail to observe Him residing in the natural order.

Emphasis on the ephemerality and non-premanence of the cosmic order is perhaps the key to the interpretation of the Guru's conception of *maya* and the world. Maya is that of which the essence is time; it has come into Being at the will of the Divine, and must disappear when He so ordains. In other words, Nature as creation is neither beginningless nor self-sufficient. It rests in the Creator, whose embodiment it is. Thus, *maya* and *qudrat* (Nature) are identical in *Gurbani*. The world of nature may be taken as maya incarnate, denying any special status or extraordinary existence to maya. Accordingly, the world is not rejected as "illusion" in the *Bani*.

In modern times, *maya* has been interpreted in several ways, departing from the exclusive meaning assigned to it by the orthodox Indian view, viz. grand illusion, giving maya an ontological status while denying reality to it. Dr Radhakrishnan is known to have distinguished phenomenality and unreality, a view that comes quite close to the Sikh view. The world is phenomenal but not unreal; it is not *real* either.

In Sikh Gurbani, maya is also equated with wealth, as also with the sense of attachment of worldly possessions. Most often, the term denotes delusion, since under the spell of maya, the mind is not able to distinguish truth from falsehood, the everlasting from the ephemeral, the essence from mere appearance. In a word, maya in Sikhism connotes *avidya*, that is, ignorance. This is the subjective dimension of maya, as opposed to the Advaitic approach that not only emphasizes the objective aspect, but leads to an overdose of objectification in its treatment of the concept. The Sikh view lays stress on the lessening of maya's spell on the human mind, so that with the liberated psychic faculties, one may attain to the state of spiritual enlightenment, - a state with no trace of maya.

Mysteries of the Cosmic Order

Philosophers and scientists, as well as spiritual visionaries are agreed on one point, that cosmology finds itself surrounded by some of the un-resolved mysteries. Is the universe finite or infinte? bounded or unbounded? Guru Nanak in his own style answered the question - "millions are the underworlds, millions float in space; despairing of the final count, the Vedas give up stake."[9] The extent of creation is not comprehended in full measure by anyone. And what the distances are like, traversed by the celestial bodies? - "In control moves the sun, in discipline moves the moon; billions of miles they travel, with no halt, no end."[10] In terms of the temporal order, no one has been able to pin-point the date of creation:

> What the hour, what the time,
> what date and day?
> Which the season, which month
> when came the cosmic play?
> Knew not the pundits time
> though given a hint in Puran;
> Knew not the qazis time, who composed the Quran;
> Nor knows the yogi time – season, month or date;
> He-himself the secret knows, who the world creates.[11]

Indian thinkers of antiquity and scientists of today, both talk in terms of the 'cosmic egg'- without solving the puzzle of its origin. Who laid the 'egg'? And when? Since the phases of expansion and contraction are beyond count or estimation, how can one speak of the first creation? "As regards the beginning," says Guru Nanak, "the best course is to admit to a sense of wonderfulness." In our times, Dr Radhakrishnan has echoed his view by proclaiming that the meaning of mystery, the origin of the world, cannot be scitifically apprehended. Expressing his faith in the absolute freedom of the Absolute Being, he avers: ''The mystery of the world abides in freedom. Freedom is the primordial source and condition of all existence; it precedes all determination.''[12] Mans's non-knowing or *avidya* is the most important meaning Dr Radhakrishnan gives to the term '*maya*'; it comes closest to the Sikh view that equates *maya* with delusion, making men overlook the divine principle operating in the created world order.

The Sikh view recognizes the principles of Hukam and Grace, bringing the living beings closer to the Creator. "Philosophically, Hukam is the apprehension of that mystery which underlies all existence, and which can express itself only in the action of submission and resignation."[13] The Sikh cosmology, based upon a profound theistic faith, finally eliminates the duality of Nature and God, existence and essence, through a formula that brings the Essence within the ambit of Existence. Guru Nanak perceives the same Light everywhere and in every heart; for him one single Essence pervades and informs the entire multiplicity of the cosmic existence. It is not a case of Essence and Existence, but simply a case of Essence-in-Existence. And Guru Amar Das exhorts man to realize the same Essence in oneself:

> You embody the very Light, O Man,
> Recognize the Essence of your life.[14]

NOTES

1. Japuji : *The Sikh Prayer*, Ed. Wazir Singh, 1982, p.31.
2. CF. Wazir Singh, *Philosophy of Sikh Religion*, Delhi : 1981, 0.45.
3. *Guru Granth* (Var Asa), p.463.
4. See *The Changing Concept of the Universe* (A.M.U., Aligarh), 1967, p.108.
5. Japuji, op.cit., p.23.
6. *Guru Granth* (Sukhmani), p.294.
7. Japuji, op.cit., p.31.
8. *Dasam Granth*, p.1387.
9. Japuji, op.cit., p.23.
10. Guru Granth (Var Asa), 0.464.
11. Japuji, op.cit.p.21.
12. Schilpp (Ed.) *The Philosophy of S.Radhakrishnan,* 1952, p.801.
13. G.S.Talib, *Guru Nanak* : *His Personality & Vision,* 1969, p.147.
14. *Guru Granth* (Asa), p.441.

THE SIKH VISION OF VALUES

The Sikh religion is a value-oriented religion. Its metaphysics is intertwined with its axiological position. Both the aspects take their expression through the medium of Guru-Granth poetry - the fountainhead of all the philosophical and spiritual thought-currents of Sikhism. Despite the fact that no cut-and-dried "theory" of values is to be found in the pages of the voluminous scripture, its poetry offers a rich fare of values ranging from the purely human to purely divine ones. A "system" of the values adumbrated in the inspired poetry of Guru Granth Sahib, has to be worked out, just as the metaphysics, epistemology, ethics and other theoretical systems are to be probed and interpreted before a philosophical superstructure is raised on its spiritual foundations.

Axiological Dimension of Sikhism

Sikhism has a pronounced axiological dimension. The Sikh spirituality is replete with numerous values, which can be classified into different sets, such as concerns and interests of the individual, values of social welfare, spiritual values and purely Divine values. Interestingly, the Guru-Granth poetry employs the term Qimat (lit. value) in the axiological as well as evaluative sense. In the latter case, it uses the expression 'qimat' as equivalent to 'measuring the value' of an entity, which in most cases is the Divine or Supreme Reality. Negatively, it suggests the idea of 'disvalue' when it castigates some entity or act as devoid of value. The most highly prized values of Sikhism are those which are believed to emanate from and reside in the Godhead. At the other extreme are disvalues that are grounded in the egocentricity of the degenerate individual.

The first indication of the values that are divine in character, is found in the basic formula of the Sikh creed, with which the scriptural text opens. Commonly known as Mul-Mantra, this initial statement lays down the metaphysical foundation of Sikhism in an aphorisitc form. All the symbols establish the monotheistic faith and refer to the dimensions of unicity and plurality, transcendence and immanence, and personal-impersonal modes of the Divine existence. Two of the symbols employed in the Mul-mantra, viz. Gur and Prasada, refer to the enlightening and gracious aspects of the Supreme Reality. Gur (or Guru) means the Enlightener, and Prasad(i) literally means Grace. These two, indicative as they are of metaphysical traits of the Absolute-cum-God, are also full of axiological import of the basic creed of Sikh religion.

Besides the *Mul-Mantra*, page after page of the voluminous (1430-page) text makes references to the numerous values embedded in the Divine Being. Some of the values lend themselves to interpretation in terms of principles, such as the principle of enlightenment, the principle of grace, the source of all creativity and artistry, the principle and source of goodness, moral excellence and love in life. All what is prized as valuable in human life intrinsically belongs to the Divine, according to the Sikh teaching. Any doctrine of values in the context of Sikhism, must take into consideration the "absolute" value forming the basis of all the other values.

The Ordering of Values

As a theistic religion, Sikhism cannot align itself with some of the classical schools of Indian thought, such as Buddhism, Jainism and Charvaka, for which 'spiritual' values do not entail the existence of a Spiritual Being. Nor can it accept the position taken by some of the contemporary systems of philosophy, e.g. Existentialism, Marxism and some brands of Humanism, which hold Man as the author of all values. For the Sikh, God is the ultimate source of values, just as He is the creator of all beings. Consequently, the Sikh theory of values would accord primacy to 'divine' values, treating human values as of secondary importance. This is in spite of the logical position that, after all, it requires *man* to posit ultimate and intrinsic values in God; it would be all 'fact' and no 'value' without man.

In the ordering of values, according to the Sikh belief, a clear hierarchy emerges, with the Divine Attributes occupying the highest place and the ideals of human life the next one. The traditional Indian conception of the Supreme Reality, namely, *Sat-Chit-Anand* (Being-Consciousness-Bliss) is assimilated in Guru Nanak's poetic expression:

> All hail to primal Source,
> the sole Creator, Power!
> He is Truth, he Beauty, spirit's Joy for ever.[1]

The formless Absolute of the Guru's conception is the inexpressible Void *(Sunya)*, or the unmanifest Spiritual Essence, or the pre-cosmic mode of Being, rapt in its own blissful 'trance'. The eternality, infinity and transcendence of such a Being are among the values which cannot be associated with human mode of existence. Similarly, creativity as the divine attribute of Creator-Person is a value of the first order, to which no human claim is thinkable.

To the second order of values belong the ideals of human life, such as enlightenment, love, aesthetic enjoyment, altruism and mystical communion. There may be a correlation between some values of the first order and those of the human order, as for instance between God as Bliss and human state of blissfulness, God as Grace and human graciousness, God as Truth and human enlightenment. The Divine Perfection as a value may not be realizable in human terms, but man's perfectibility is certainly a value worthy of promotion in life. Man may not aspire to be God, but he may legitimately aspire to inculcate values that are godly.

The Supreme Value in Sikhism

The symbols '*Naad*' and 'Veda' frequently employed in the Guru-Granth compositions, should serve as the key to a doctrine of the supreme value in Sikhism. Naad literally means sound, a vibration arising from the striking of a musical organ etc. and received at the auditory receptors. Figuratively, it means harmony, though again based upon the concept of harmonious sound of music. In mystical sense, 'naad' is unstruck melody, that is, not produced by any organ, yet 'heard' in one's mind. The figure *anahad naad*, a favourite of the yogis, find its echo in the Bani, implying a spiritual state of communication with the highest Being. It is an experience of oneness with the supreme reality, free of all duality and discordance, and experience of harmony between the human soul and the cosmic spirit. Such intimate union is the goal of all mysticism, the "drop" merging with the "ocean" of Being, attaining to the ideal state of harmony.

The other of the pair of symbols, 'veda' implies wisdom. In the religious context, it is spiritual illumination, or enlightenment of the most exalted kind. Since the concept is intrinsically related to the Vedas, the holy books containing highest wisdom, the epistemological significance of 'veda' cannot be lost sight of. The Indian tradition holds the Vedas as the source of all knowledge, enlightenment and direction of the mind and soul of man. A philosopher, in love with wisdom, takes recourse to study and reflection, - the vedic pursuit. The yogi adopts the practice of "listening" to the *naad.* In the Sikh view, both the courses of 'naad' and 'veda', of harmony and wisdom, as delineated in Gurbani, pave the way of life leading to the ultimate goal in terms of Guru's Word.

The supreme value in Sikhism is termed *Abhedata* (merger, harmony), as well as *Brahman-gyan* (absolute knowledge). Do both of these suggest the same value, or a set of two values? The disciple of Ten Gurus, faithfully following the spiritual direction of Gurbani, undergoes an experience of spiritual merging, which at the same time gives him a quintessence of the absolute reality. The experience and the illumination are two facets of the same single occurrence. The experience of merging (*abhedata*) is the mystical dimension of the value that is wisdom (*gyan*) of the highest order,– the epistemological aspect of inward experience. This supreme value of Sikhism has also been characterized as *jivan-mukti* (emancipation-in-life), synthesizing in itself both the "naad" and the "veda".

Humanistic Values

Values that are important from human point of view are those associated with human welfare at various levels. The divine order of values is doubtlessly the higher order, encompassing infinity and eternality, cosmic creativity and transcendence, perfection and sovereignty, omniscience and grace. The Absolute-God of Sikhism is beyond all attributes (*Nirgun*), unrivalled and formless; yet He is present in all the wordly forms and qualities. Since all these values are beyond the reach of finite, temporal and imperfect beings, the most significant values for humanity are values of the human order, encompassing survival values, socio-ethical and intellectual values, aesthetic and spiritual values. This is the order of humanistic values, geared to the promotion of physical and mental health of the individual, reconstitution of human faculties, love of God and service of man.

Sikhism, while it recognizes the four-fold order of traditional values (viz. Dharma, Artha, Kama and Moksha) as a broad framework, does not attach much of significance to renunciation and asceticism, or to the ideal of *sanyas*. Instead, it favours the value of non-attachment (*nirlepata*), that is, leading the normal life of a householder with its attendant duties, without engrossing onself in passions, intemperance, and infatuation. Another value favoured by Sikhism is equipoise, the balanced life of *sehaj*, coupled with ecstasy or wonderfulness (*vismada*). Fortified by the values of ideal human life in terms of individual excellence, the disciple participates in the life of the community with the vision of well – being of the entire mankind (*sarbatt da bhala*).[2] This certainly is the loftiest of social values, most comprehensive and utilitarian in sweep. As a value of the human order, it is matched by the value of Divine Grace at the other end of the spectrum.

A System of Values in Sikhism

All the values of Sikhism, belonging to both the human and divine orders, may be arranged in the hieararchical system. Of course, the absolute value, the Divine itself, would occupy the most basic as also the most exalted place in the system, yet in the ascending order the values tend to conform to the pattern as under:

(a) Physico-economic values. - Fulfilment of the organic and emotional needs of the individual is covered by this category. Health is a value of the physical order, accorded due place in the Bani. The Gurus' philosophy of "body", treating it as the sacred abode of the spirit, marks it out from the conventional approach of relegating the body to an inferior place, with some of the ascetic schools recommending austerities and torturing of the body as a way to salvation. Another aspect of this value is comprehension of the principle governing the physical universe (laws of nature) and the human world (Karma or the moral law).[3]

(b) Intellectual values. - Knowledge and wisdom are the key-concepts of this realm, where reason (*vivek*) plays the pivotal role and Truth is the highest value. Illumination of the mind, dawning of the consciousness of an endless process of creation, philosophical realization of the immensity and plurality of cosmic existence, coupled with intuitive awareness of the non-dual nature of Reality, constitute the values of rational order.[4]

(c) Aesthetic values. - Bhakti or loving devotion to the Lord-Creator is in itself an aesthetic experience, generating the ecstatic state of bliss or *anand.* God himself is epitomized as Anand, interpreted in terms of blissful Freedom and sovereign Will. Enjoyment of God, of the grandeur and beauty of his creation, is the key to the values of aesthetic realm, which cover appreciation of creative arts, taste for poetry and music, and sense for harmony.[5]

(d) Ethical values. - Virtue is the norm of the ethical realm of values accorded a place of honour in the Sikh value-system. Its expressions are valour and purity of conduct, realization of the Divine presence in all beings and dedication to the human community.[6] Social commitment and selfless service constitute the Path of Action that represents the moral dimension of values, indispensable for the final communion.

(e) Spiritual values. - Salvation, variously interpreted as cessation of the cycle of transmigration, attainment of the beatific vision, and realization of oneness with the ground of one's being, is the ideal most often put forward by sages and savants of religion. Sikhism too presents the value of salvation in terms of *mukti* and *nirvan*,[7] but lays greatest stress on emancipation-in-life through Divine Grace. Its other dimension is spiritual harmony or merging with the Supreme Being, the absolute of all values in Sikhism.

NOTES

1. Japuji : *The Sikh Prayer*, Ed. Wazir Singh, 1982, p.37
2. The formal Sikh prayer ends with this phrase.
3. Cf. Japuji, stanza 34.
4. Japuji (stanza 35) refers to the Realm of Knowledge.
5. Cf. Guru Nanak's verse in Var Srang, *Guru Granth*, p.1246.
6. Japuji (first part of stanza 37) refers to the Realm of Action.
7. Nirvan is often written as *Nirbaan* in Gurbani and refers to the ideal state of being.

THE SIKH VIEW OF KNOWLEDGE

In a sense, knowledge is the foremost concern of Sikhism. The Sikh way of life is shaped by the teachings contained in the scriptural compositions, which in turn place before man the ideal of 'perfect' knowledge one is capable of realizing. The 'Sikh' is a disciple, a learner, a seeker, even in the literal sense of the term. His inmost quest is to acquire the knowledge that the Gurus impart for human salvation; and on acquisition of such knowledge he discovers that knowledge itself is salvation. The Indian term *jnan* (gyan/gian) primarily implies spiritual awareness, even though 'gyan' (like 'experience' and 'knowledge') may be employed in a variety of meanings extending from the most trivial to most sacred. In the context of Sikh philosophy, Gyan in the ordinary sense of knowledge has its own place, but its use in the heightened sense of divine knowledge is underlined, at times by compounding it with another term, resulting in the formation such as Brahman-Gyan, Gyan-Khand and the like.

Foundations of Sikh Epistemology

A logically fashioned theory of knowledge may not readily be available in the religious literature of Sikhism, but adequate foundations of such a theory may well be located in the compositions of Guru Granth Sahib, supplemented by the Dasam Granth. The early interpreters and scholars were not interested in the propounding of epistemological formulations, except in favouring a sort of mystical-intuitional approach to the apprehension of divine reality. It is under the influence of modern philosophy that some of the contemporary interpreters have turned their attention to the problem of knowledge from the Sikh perspective. It may be conceded, however, that in spite of the inspiration provided by Western philosophy, researchers have linked the epistemological bearings of the Guru Granth hymns with the classical formulations of Indian philosophy.

The Sikh epistemology is one with the general Indian approach that knowledge of the scriptural texts enlightens the mind, dispelling darkness and delusion. The Indian tradition invests the term 'Veda' with the meaning of wisdom, transcendent awareness and knowledge divine. Guru Nanak employs the same term to symbolize enlightenment of the human spirit, even as he rejects the Vedic literature in its anecdotal and ceremonial aspects. The part of the Vedas that enlists the support of the Gurus relates to the metaphysical import of the text with its soteriological implications. Guru Angad, the second in succession to Guru Nanak, holds the hymns of the latter as the immortalizing words that express the "essence" rather than peripheral issues.[1] Guru Amar Das, the third Guru, refers to the contemplative aspect *(Nam)* that stands out in the Vedas but is overlooked by the ignorant behaving like eccentrics.[2]

Another concept basic to the epistemological position of Sikhism is Sabad (*sabda*, sound or word). Indian philosophy with its numerous stages and schools, lays down a number of categories of knowledge (*pramanas*), viz. perception, inference, analogy, *arthapatti* (postulation), *abhava* (absence), besides *sabda* (testimony). The category of Testimony, in referring to knowledge of supersensible realities, poses problems of God, soul, immortality etc. on the 'authority' of sages and seers. To the Sikh, this authority is represented by the Guru, who is the spiritual teacher or mentor of the faith. For Guru Nanak, the divine word comes as a 'revelation', inspiring him to utter words constituting poetic outpourings. Interpreted in matter-of-fact language, the verbal testimony of Guru-Bani (the Gurus' hymns) stands for the expression of a mystical mood. Guru in communion with the Godhead undergoes an experience that is ineffable, but the teacher in him inspires him to address mankind, to express the inexpressible in the form of linguistic symbols of poesy, or musical thought as it were. No wonder that every syllable, every word and every hymn in the Guru Granth is described as 'sabad' (pronounced *shabad*) by the Sikh community.

Sources and Types of Knowledge

The ultimate source of verbal testimony, i.e. *sabad*, in terms of the Sikh faith, is the inscrutable mystery of Divine Reality intuitively experienced by the rarest of human individuals. 'Sabad' in the exalted sense refers to the Ultimate, the Absolute or the Formless Brahman. It has been given the epithets of *Sabda-Brahman* and *Sabda-Guru*. The Indian tradition equates it with AUM (i.e. *Oam*) which is treated as the holiest of sounds. Converted into a linguistic symbol, the sound Aum takes the form of Oam, the letter. Guru Nanak has employed its variations, e.g. Onam and Oamkaar, in his compositions.[3] The symbol Oam has undergone a slight modification in orthography in the Sikh scripture, and is most often preceded by the numeral 1 (one), the whole compound reading 'Ek Oamkaar' (One Supreme Lord). The significance of *sabada-pramana* in the Sikh epistemology is thus evident.

Apart from testimony, the Gurus recognized other categories of knowledge as well, according due place to each. In one of the hymns, Guru

Arjan refers to the various sensory media of perception[4] : "Let us meditate on the name of God internally; with the tongue repeat the Divine Name; with the eyes look at the manifest Divine; with the ears listen to the Holy Name; absorbed in the love of the Lord, let us attain to salvation." Sense perception does play its part in the religious affairs of man, even though empiricism as the exclusive theory of knowledge does not find favour with religious leaders and thinkers. Nor does rationalism pure and simple satisfy religion, even if reason is accorded a place of honour in its scheme of things. The Sikh scripture time and again refers to an intelligent and rational approach to matters ethical and spiritual. The term *budhi-vivek* (reason) is a favourite expression with the authors of Guru-Granth hymns. But, neither perception nor thought alone would serve the ends of religion. The spiritual life, particularly of the Sikh, is to be guided by the light of reason coupled with intuitive insight. The "eyes" that "see" my Lord, are made of "different" stuff,[5] avers Guru Nanak. If at all, it requires "perception" of a higher order.

Sense, intellect and intuition form parts of the process that furnishes knowledge to the individual. The sources being different (viz. the empirical world, conceptual world, and spiritual world), the types of knowledge so furnished tend to be different too, though the process itself is one single whole. In fact, two or more media are coordinated in the process of knowledge : the senses providing raw-materials and the intellect, power that shapes the material into end-product. One without the other is helpless. The role of intuition is to unify the elements of knowledge and to enlighten the self. Its insights lead one to have glimpses of the higher reaches of reality ordinarily hidden from view. These are the glimpses that constitute mystical awareness and produce state of aesthetic enjoyment, ecstasy or blissfulness. It is in such a mood that one discerns transcendent orders of reality, at the same time immanent in the phenomenal world:

> I perceive Thy form in all life and light;
> I realize Thy power in all spheres and sight.[6]

The Ideal of Knowledge

The Sikhs were traditionally called the circle of *gyanis*[7]. A *gyani* is a knowledgeable, learned person; one who knows more than the ordinary folks do; one who has succeeded in acquiring the secrets of creation and the Creator, through sustained study of scriptural/theological texts, generally under the guidance of a competent teacher. Gyanis among the Sikh community had a tradition of interpreting the Guru Granth compositions to the people, of leading a disciplined life that influenced others, and of devoting themselves to study, often by way of avocation. The epithet 'gyani' was a mark of honour, though lately it has shed much of its luster. In the eyes of Guru Nanak, learning when truly contemplated, makes one a benefactor of all.[8] The dimension of altruism in the make-up of a learned person is unmistakable here. Yet another dimension was added by Guru Tegh Bahadur, the ninth mentor, when he defined the 'gyani' as one who neither oppresses anyone, nor tolerates oppression, neither frightens others nor is afraid of anyone.[9] Knowledge gives him the power to effectively deal with the world, and to conduct himself reasonably, with malice towards none.

Perferction of man in terms of knowledge is an ideal not possible to realize, since the frontiers of knowledge keep on receding. But, knowledge here means 'scientific' knowledge and perfection is merely technical perfection. When religion speaks of perfect knowledge, it postulates human perfectibility in terms of divine knowledge. Once the 'key' is grasped, the secret is laid bare. The Sikh epistemology places before man the ideal of knowledge that is within the reach of everyone who follows the discipline, but is actually realized by the elect (if not the elite). Sikhism talks of the spiritual perfectibility of man, which takes into account disciplined effort on the seeker's part and bestowal of grace on the Divine's part. The 'guru' in the human form acts as a go-between, imparting instruction as to the path to be adopted, and revealing the spiritual light. This duty of the 'guru' is performed by the Bani (words/compositions) providing enlightenment to the aspiring disciple. For the Sikh, Guru's Bani is 'guru' itself. Its message is to be deciphered and followed. Reading the message is one form of knowledge, acquisition of the secret revealed in the message is another and the ideal form.

The ideal of knowledge, according to Gurbani, is Truth. In abstract terms, the truth of Guru Nanak's vision is the Absolute, or the formless, undifferentiated reality; in theological terms, the same truth is presented as the True One, the divine Being, creator and protector of the universe. Gurbani employs Truth in both the senses. In defining 'Brahman-gyani' (lit. knower of the Absolute), Guru Arjan depicts him as one who has the True Being in the mind and the True One on the tongue; who perceives not aught other than the One.[10] Not that the cosmic forms disappear for the seer, only his vision encompasses the entire existence as manifest Being. He is enabled, as it were, to look at the inmost depths or 'secrets' of reality. An individual endowed with such a superb insight, who has nothing concealed from his spiritual eyes, is characterized, apart from Brahman-gyani, as the Gurmukh (god-oriented), in the text. In one of the verses, the Gurmukh is described by Guru Amar Das as one who never gets senile, because of his internal light; who always enjoys praising his Lord's merits, with enduring contemplation in the mind; to whom only the One Being appears as immanent in all the hearts.[11] It is not simply cosmic consciousness that is implied by the ideal of Brahman-gyan, it is the *absolute* consciousness that is meant.

Sikh Mysticism

A visionary attaining to the status of Brahman-gyani may conveniently be characterized as a mystic. The mystical emotion, or simply mystic insight, is differentiated from mysticism as a formal cult, in the Sikh tradition. Sikhism recognizes no faith other than the one inculcated by Guru-Granth poetry. It does not accept mysticism as a formal creed, requiring a prescribed code of penances, austerities or techniques of concentration, coupled with asceticism or complete withdrawal from the world. Nor does it subscribe to a philosophy of quietism that goes with mysticism. The only sense in which mysticism can be associated with Sikhism is the inspiration born of inner illumination, preparing the individual for a life of dedication and social commitment. "There is no reason for denying the existence of experiences that are called mystical." Sikhism fully shares this belief of John Dewey.[12] "For the mystics, the essential feature of religion is its inner quality. Doctrines, observances, institutions are secondary, and if unduly stressed, they may become a positive hindrance to the life of the spirit."[13]

The Sikh mysticism draws its sustenance from the mystical emotion, without which the feelings that are prized in life would be out of the question, for it is the mystical emotion that generates a faith to live by. As the individual develops and becomes maturer, the emotion becomes deeper and indicates the course he will adopt in proportion to the amount of contemplation practised. Mysticism in such an aspect is rather indispensable for the religious life. The other type is the methodological aspect, the technique of capturing moments of thrill and mystical vision of reality. The danger here is that one may practise mysticism for the thrill and not for the truth; the real blessing may be sacrificed for the sake of mere frenzy. In the final analysis, it is the noetic quality of mysticism that brings fulfilment. The mystic is involved in a relation of love with the ulitmate Being who is perceived as beyond the self as also within it, a God who hides Himself as well as reveals Himself. According to Sikh faith, it is not the prerogative of prophets and holy men alone to have the mystical vision of reality, but it is well within the reach of all who care.[14] If it could inspire the lives of large numbers in a generation, we would be able to hope for the creation of a society of Brahman-gyanis as visualized by Guru Nanak, or a society of gnostic beings, as contemplated more recently by Sri Aurobindo, the mystic-philosopher of our day.

Restructuring of Human Faculties

Whether it is intuition and mystic insight, or sensory perception and reasoning, one or another human faculty is involved in the process of generating knowledge. The quality and status of knowledge would depend upon the faculty, or combination of faculties, employed. The genius of exceptionally gifted individuals produces ideas and makes discovery of truths that inspire awe in the ordinary minds. Mystics too refer to realms beyond the reach of lesser mortals. The question arises, can the common range of intelligence turn into high genius, and can any of the ordinary people aspire to enjoy the ecstatic thrill of mysticism? Whereas a positive answer to the first part is doubtful, the sages and saints of religion assure the inquisitive followers that mystical communication is a distinct possibility for every one of them. The position taken by Sikhism nearly supports this claim, the only reservation being the part played by divine Grace, which itself remains a mystery.

"The blessings are in the hands of the Lord; no pleading with Him succeeds. Those who remain awake (in expectation), may fail to receive, while others may be aroused from slumbers to have the blessing." -- This is how Guru Nanak responds to Sheikh Farid's exhortation that the devotees constantly keep vigil in order not to miss the moment of blessing.[15] Human endeavour is a must, but is not sufficient in itself; the reward may not be in proportion to the effort made. The Gurus did advocate a life of activity, of endeavour, of conquest over the forces of ignorance, superstition and hypocrisy. Enlightenment at the worldly and the spiritual levels was one of the ends of life recommended by them. Yet, they insisted, human effort is supplemented by the will and grace of the Divine, who is the supreme Enlightener of mankind. Human faculties are marked by limitations, so is human knowledge imperfect and partial. For overcoming the limits and errors of knowledge, man needs to evolve his faculties and somehow restructure his capabilities.

In this respect, Sikh epistemology holds out hope for mankind. Guru Nanak gives a poetic transcript of the mystically intuited realms of spirituality, in his celebrated composition 'Japuji'. In the third of the Five Realms known as Saram Khand, the Guru makes an allusion to the Realm of Creativity with its key-note of 'form': where structures are uniquely forged and conform to the highest norm. "All what is fashioned here, defies expression, speech. If in rashness someone tried, shall he come to grief./Here are faculties reconstituted, knowing, thinking, mind, intellect:/Consciousness of angels, mystics, is moulded here afresh."[16] When blessed with Grace, the spiritual endeavours of someone start bearing fruit; when he is admitted into the realm of ecstasy and enabled to transcend the partiality and imperfection of his native faculties, he acquires absolutely new vision of reality. At this stage, knowledge blazes with splendour; "wondrous visions, melodious sounds and million joys" accompany the enlightenment that descends upon the blessed soul.[17]

NOTES

1. *Guru Granth,* p.1243.
2. *Guru Granth* (Anand), p.919.
3. See *Guru Granth* (Ramakali Onkar), pp.929-30.
4. *Guru Granth* (Var Gujri), p.517.
5. *Guru Granth* (Vad-hans), p.577; (Var Maru), p.1100.
6. *Guru Granth* (Asa), p.351.
7. See S.S.Kaveeshar, *Sikh Dharam Darshan,* Patiala, 1969, p.3.
8. *Guru Granth* (Asa), p.356.
9. *Guru Granth,* p.1427.
10. *Guru Granth* (Sukhmani), p.272.
11. *Guru Granth,* p.1418.
12. John Dewey, *A Common Faith*, 1934.
13. Sydney Spencer, *Mysticism in World Religion*, 1966, Chap.9.
14. Cf. Wazir Singh, *Hamnaism of Guru Nanak,* Delhi, 1977, p.153.
15. *Guru Granth,* p.83; p.1384.
16. Japuji : *The Sikh Prayer*, Ed. Wazir Singh, 1982, p.37.
17. Ibid..

THE ENLIGHTENER'S PATH
(A perspective on Gurmat)

A term unique and peculiar to Sikhism, *Gurmat* has a wide semantic range. It covers doctrinal, prescriptive and directional aspects of the Sikh faith and praxis. In its applicability, the term refers primarily to the basic tenets, principles and theological structure of Sikh religion, as derived from the teachings of Guru Nanak and his nine successors. The term further refers to the Sikh way of life both in its individual and social expressions, largely conforming to the tradition evolved during the five centuries of Sikh history. In additon, *Gurmat* refers to the institutions set up by the Gurus and the Sikh community, for the day-to-day guidance of adherents. In any exigency, the decision to be taken by the followers must conform to Gurmat in its ideological and/or conventional sense.

In its formulation, Gurmat combines the elements of *guru* (spiritual teacher) and *mat* (instruction). The 'guru' in this context means the Ten Gurus in person as well as Guru-Bani. The instruction of the Guru implies the teaching imparted through the compositions enshrined in the Guru Granth, and the orientation provided by the Gurus to their disciples. The Sikh community derives all its direction for the conduct of life, both in the sacred and secular spheres, from this fundamental source, supplemented, of course, by its exegetical literature. The teaching imparted by the Gurus for human salvation, for the conduct of a pious and virtuous life in society, and for meeting the challenges facing the individual and the community from time to time, is collectively given the epithet of Gurmat.

The part of Gurmat that primarily deals with the doctrinal issues of the faith, is known as Gurdarshan (lit. philosophy of the Gurus). Technically speaking, this precisely is the theology of Sikhism, since Gurdarshan takes upon itself the task of explicating and defending, in a systematic manner, the thematic issues involved in the Gurus' teaching. It argues the case of Sikhism, with a view to establishing its excellence as a religious philosophy, without however denigrating parallel systems. Its critial approach is confined to the rejection of purely mythical, superstitious and ritualistic aspects of other faiths, which according to Gurmat are not worthy of pursuit. In its constructive approach, Gurdarshan respects the essence of ethico-spiritual teachings of all religious traditions, in their endeavour to serve the cause of human welfare and salvation.

Sikh philosophy builds upon the base provided by Gurmat and Gurdarshan. It extends the ratiocinative activity of Gurdarshan by the application of techniques perfected by philosophy and theology. In the process, it has ventured into the area of modern hermeneutics, and stimulated the growth of creative interpretation of Sikhism. It has an open-minded approach both to the Indian and Western traditions of theological and philosophical thought, and does not fight shy of enriching its expositions by the resources and logical tools advanced by them. Yet, it makes endeavour to remain a functionally independent discipline, with its own doctrinal identity and sovereignty.

In its theological ramifications, Gurmat encompasses a strict monotheistic belief, coupled with an idealistic metaphysics. Faith in the spiritual Being, as supreme reality without attributes, is the starting point of Gurdarshan. But the personal, attributed nature of the Supreme Being is the other side of the coin. Sikhism posits creativity as one of the cardinal attributes of the Absolute-cum-God of its conception. The Creative Spirit brings about the universe at will, without needing the services of agencies like Brahma or other deities of the classical Indian thought. Man, as the pinnacle of creation, is born with a divine spark; his salvation lies in the recognition of his own spiritual essence and immanence of the Divine in the cosmic creation. Fulfilment comes with the promotion, in one's life, of values comprising harmony, enlightenment and bliss on the one hand, and universal welfare of humanity on the other.

The way of life prescribed by Gurmat consists in cultivating faith in the teachings of Gurbani, acquisition of higher mode of consciousness, resigning oneself to the will divine, and performing duties assigned by tradition. The first act suggested by Gurmat is prayer in its various dimensions. Prayer is said by the Sikh in all situations of life. It may be in the form of recitation of Gurbani, or the formal corporate prayer, or silent contemplation in one's solitude. Secondly, Gurmat has evolved a tradition of observances and ceremonies for the followers of Sikh faith, which are simplified version of the complex and elaborate rituals of the Hindu society. Gurmat recognizes no priestly class as such; any devoted Sikh may lead the prayer, perform the wedding ceremony known as Anand Karaj, or recite compositions from the Guru Granth at a congregation. The rites of passage, viz. ceremonies connected with the birth of a baby, initiation, marriage and death, all are performed in the 'presence' of the Guru, that is, the holy Word picked at random from the scripture, followed by collective prayer and distribution of pudding (*karah-prasad*). Recital of six stanzas from the *Anand* (Bliss) is mandatory on all occasions, of joy or sorrow, wedding or death.

On the ethical plane, Gurmat prescribes a code of duties and moral virtues, coupled with a discipline of puritan nature for the Khalsa. The latter is so designated when a disciple joins the special brotherhood after going through the baptism of Amrit and taking vows of do's and don'ts. Violation of any part of the code (particularly the four taboos) of the Khalsa is not only treated as disregard of Gurmat, but renders the offender liable to penalty and punishment. The Tribunal of Akal Takht at Amritsar has traditionally been regarded as supreme in the social and secular affairs of the Sikhs, as also the authority to issue edicts, and to excommunicate a member, if and when necessary.

Under the directional province of Gurmat fall injuctions and counsels, guidance and advice offered to individuals and groups in times of crisis, etc. Normally, the power to offer solutions to problems posed, vests in the five elect ones. At times, one 'consults' the Guru by approaching the Guru Granth with prayer for guidance and help and the 'command' comes in the form of the *word* (*sabad*, verse or stanza). The Gurmat tradition is replete with instances when the community leaders decided on a course, political or otherwise, through recourse to such consultation. The institutions of Gurmata (sacred resolution), decision by majority vote or unanimity (*bahu-samiti or sarb-samiti*), executive council and assembly (*panj piyare* and *sangat*/ congregation) date back to the late seventeenth and early eighteenth centuries.

Some of the lingering controversies have been resolved by Gurmat through the establishment of conventions, or even by adopting postures of silence or acquiescence. In regard to the wedding ceremony, the convention of *anand karaj* led to enactment of Anand Marriage Act in 1909. The remnants of idol-worship were removed during the Gurdwara reform movement. The 48 hour non-stop reading of the Guru Granth, popularly known as *akhand paath*, has over the decades come to be accepted as part of the Sikh way of life. As regards meat-eating, Gurmat has not issued a final verdict, both vegetarianism and non-vegetarianism being current with sections of the community. Casteism is ruled out in principle, but caste-names are freely used by vast sections of the Sikhs, in order to perpetuate family identities, etc.

Gurmat, in its various connotations, presents a conceptual-cum-social framework for the Sikh. Every child in the family picks up the Sikh idiom and phraseology and takes to the custom of paying obeisance to the Guru Granth and joining in the formal prayer. The Sikh mode of dress and daily discipline come quite naturally to the adult, even if considerable amount of flexibility is encountred in the sartorial and eating habits, life styles and so on. Free-will is exercised in various matters, including some of those falling within the set tradition and custom. For instance, liberty is taken with the naming-ceremony; with *daswandh* (setting apart one-tenth of income for socio-religious causes); with the injuction of sharing one's food with the needy; with the routine of absorbing oneself in *nam-simran* (holy contemplation) at day-break, dusk and bed-time.

The Sikh is persuaded against renunciation. Gurmat makes a departure from the Indian tradition of attaching highest value to Sannyas, the last in the scheme of four stages of life. According to Gurmat, the householder's life is best; it affords ample opportunity for developing virtues of compassion and non-attachment while performing one's worldly chores. The family-life led with sense of duty; earning one's livelihod through honest means, avoiding avarice and deceit, and remaining loyal to one's family and associates, is rated higher and nobler than renunciation, even as reverence for the pious and saintly is taken for granted. Parasitism is forbidden by Gurmat. Use of intoxicants is frowned upon. Instead, cultivation of finer tastes in life, particularly interest in music, is highly recommended. No doubt, the Sikh tradition has evolved its own style of singing Gurbani with the accompaniment of music, known as *kirtan.*

Efforts at the interpretation of Gurmat for the general public started during the lifetime of Guru Nanak himself, when his son Baba Sri Chand founded his Udasi sect. However systematic exposition of Gurmat principles was initiated by Bhai Gurdas. These efforts were directed towards the defining of Gurmukh, the God-oriented one, in terms of Guru's teaching, besides evolving an exegetical framework for Gurbani. The interpretive process continued under the supervision of stalwarts like Bhai Mani Singh, and culminated in the Singh Sabha movement which produced interpreters of the stature of Bhai Vir Singh, Bhai Jodh Singh, Professor Teja Singh and Professor Sahib Singh, during the twentieth century.

THE SIKH VISION OF PEACE

The Sikh religion stands for peace, without advocating pacifism as a cult or creed. The Sikh tradition dating from the fifteenth century has been characterized, on the one hand, by spiritual pursuit tempered with ethical conduct of a puritan nature, and by intermittent struggle to maintain the identity of the community, on the other. To strive for peace inwardly, and to fight for the maintenance of social identity against political odds, has been the lot of the Sikhs ever since the time of Guru Nanak (1469-1539). His nine successors, until the departure of the Tenth Guru from the scene (A.D. 1708), nurtured the community on the spiritual-cum-social path indicated by Guru Nanak. During the testing time, the eighteenth centrury to be precise, the community bereft of the guidance and leadership of the Gurus in person, faced grim struggles, constant battles and persecution, with rare fortitude born of the inspiration provided by the Gurus' teachings. The pivot around which the Sikhs moved in their adversity, as they always do in comfort and joy as well, is the scripture *Guru Granth Sahib*, enshrining (in its 1430 pages) the wisdom and revealed word in the form of poetic compositions of six Gurus and thirty like-minded devotees and men of piety.

Formation of Sikh Character

In order to appreciate fully the contribution of the Sikhs to the cause of peace, it would be helpful to cast a glance at the tradition of Sikh character and psyche. Professor Pritam Singh, a contemporary academician of repute, with liberal outlook, discusses the issues of Sikh identity and mental make-up. "Members of the Sikh community carry their badge of identity so naturally and prominently on their persons that it is not difficult to identify them even in a crowd." He argues that during the post-Guru Gobind Singh period, "the socio-psychological differences among Muslims and Sikhs were so marked... that the Sikhs had no fear of wholesale absorption from that side, but there was so much social kinship between Hindus and Sikhs that the Sikh minority often felt the threat of submersion in the religious majority. Even today, anyone who cuts off his hair is automatically considered to have relapsed into the Hindu mass."[1]

As for the persecution of the Sikhs at the hands of the Mughal ruling circles and invaders from the neighbouring Muslim states, Professor Pritam Singh quotes Qazi Nur Mohammad, historian, who "showers all sorts of abuses on the Sikhs, but speaks highly of their fighting skill." The Qazi, in his *Jang Nama* (1765) has this to say: "In no case would they slay a coward or put any obstacle in the way of the fugitive. They do not plunder the wealth and ornaments of a woman, be she a well-to-do lady, or a maid servant. There is no adultery amongst these dogs, nor are these mischievous people given to thieving." The Professor remarks: "The indiscriminate indulgence of the Government in horrible acts of violence brought out the best that one could hope for Sikh character... The ill-clad, half-starved Sikhs, outlawed in their own homeland, kept their spirits high by indulging in the playful pastime of adding very interesting new semantic dimensions to their existing vocabulary." By all the devices available, these 'guerilla fighters' tried to preserve their individual and corporate identity.[2]

The Mughal Emperor, Bahadur Shah, "who had ascended the Delhi throne with the help of the Sikhs," had on 10th December, 1710 (a couple of years after the demise of Guru Gobind Singh) issued an Imperial Ordinance to the effect that "Every Sikh, wherever he is found, wherever he is seen, should be put to death without any hesitation and without any further thought." Lt. Col. Gulcharan Singh (Retd), in his recent write-up on Banda Singh Bahadur, the commander of the Sikh armies of the period, quotes from the *Ruqaat* of Nawab Amin-ud-Daula to say that Banda Singh did not oppress the Muslims; he only opposed tyranny and usurpation of political power which belonged to the people. "For any Muslim who approaches him, he fixes a daily allowance and wages and looks after him. He has permitted them to read *Khutba* and *Namaz*. As such, five thousand Muslims have gathered around him." Banda Singh "never harmed a woman or a child." "He did loot the nobles' property but then distributed it all among his followers, keeping nothing for himself." "At the time of his execution, when given a choice between Islam and death, he opted for the latter."[3] One of the points that emerge from the above, is the liberal-minded approach of the Sikh commander to the religion of his persecutors.

Peaceful Resistance of Oppression

The third decade of twentieth century provided a few instances of exemplary fortitude displayed by the Sikhs, in the face of brutal oppression perpetrated by the British rulers of India. The occasion was the struggle for liberation of Sikh temples, known as Gurudwara Reform Movement, spearheaded by the Akali leadership of the community. At a number of places, the Sikh masses were massacred by the *mahants* (abbots) in occupation of the shrines, with the active cooperation of the police. Reference to an instance will suffice. "At Guru-ka-Bagh, twenty kilometers from Amritsar, Sikhs' capacity for suffering and resistance was put to further trial," says Professor Harbans Singh. "The Sikhs displayed unique powers of self-control and resolution, and bore the bodily torment in a spirit of complete resignation. None of them winced or raised his hand."[4] The Rev. C. F. Andrews, who visited Amritsar and gave graphic description of the passive resistance of the Akalis, has been quoted at length by Harbans Singh. A few excerpts are given here:

"The brutality and inhumanity of the whole scene was indescribably increased by the fact that the men who were hit were praying to God and had already taken a vow that they would remain silent and peaceful in word and deed. ...A new lesson in moral warfare has been taught to the world... The blows were received one by one without resistance and without a sign of fear."[5] This happened in August, 1922. A few months earlier, the Sikhs had succeeded in retrieving the keys of the *toshakhana* (treasury-cum-museum) situated in the premises of Golden Temple at Amritsar, from the British rulers. The national leader, Mahatma Gandhi, sent this telegraphic message to the Sikh leader, Baba Kharak Singh: "The first decisive battle for independence won. Congratulations."[6] The Sikh struggle for wresting control of their holy places from the corrupt *mahants*, was in keeping with the spirit of non-violent resistance (*satyagrah*) advocated by Gandhi.

The political turn to the religious movement has been termed by the historians as the Sikhs' fight for India's freedom. Says Dr Gopal Singh: "The Sikhs launched the Gurdwara Reform Movement, which though initially aimed at purging the Sikh Shrines of the corrupt practices of their hereditary custodians, ended up in politicalizing the masses against the Government, and making the Sikhs the vanguard of freedom movement." The Congress Party passed resolutions congratulating them on the unexampled bravery of the Akalis who had set a great and noble example of non-violence for the benefit of the whole nation. Continues Gopal Singh: "There was now a complete and wholly appreciative understanding of the Sikh ethos throughout the country. Their none-too-happy image as a war-like people gave way to their being dedicated and peaceful warriors of God, spiritually awakened, highly catholic and cooperative in outlook, ready to dare and die for all good causes (and not only their own) which brought the whole country glory and honour."[7]

It was in 1925 that the British Government passed the Gurdwara Act and met the demands of the Sikhs. Gandhi was elated with their victory. He commented: The Gurdwara Act "has required the self-immolation of hundreds of the bravest in the land. It has required the imprisonment of brave Akalis. The public is familiar with their tale of suffering in jails, such marvellous sacrifice could not go in vain.''[8]

Spirit of Sacrifice and Martyrdom

The noted journalist-author Rajinder Puri observes that the Sikhs as a community were influenced by the enviornment created by Mahatma Gandhi during the early decades of the century. Their leadership was perfectly non-violent, even though it "was criticised by sections of Sikh extremists, ...who were unable to reconcile themselves to non-violent methods." Despite all this peaceful agitation, "an impression in the rest of India is allowed to persist to this day that the Punjab dragged its feet in the quest for freedom, and the Punjabis were more pro-British than the rest. The truth was the other way round." Rajinder Puri proceeds to prove his point with the help of statistics:

"Out of 2175 Indian martyrs for freedom, 1557, or 75% were Sikhs. Out of 2646 Indians sent to the Andamans for life-imprisonment 2147, or 80%, were Sikhs. Out of 127 Indians who were hanged 92, or 80%, were Sikhs. Out of 20000 who joined the Indian National Army under Subhash Bose, 1200, or 60%, were Sikhs. And the Sikhs comprise only 2% of India's total population.''

"Clearly the Sikhs, and for that matter Punjabis generally, do not require a certificate for patriotism from the rest of India."

What the community desired and insisted upon was a situation "wherein the Sikhs can also experience the glow of freedom" (phrase used by Prime Minister Nehru). As regards the 1984 events, Rajinder Puri observes: "The Sikhs were submitted to Operation Bluestar, a military assault on the Golden Temple, which most non-partisan observers concede would have been avoidable if the Government had not deliberately encouraged a situation of critical dimensions to develop for no more than electoral considerations." His conclusion is succint and to the point: "It is in the light of this background that the post-independence crisis of the Punjab must necessarily be viewed."[9] Curiously enough, the media's focus has been peripheral mode of struggle against the Establishment since 1984 days; but aberrations are aberrations. The core of Punjab problem has been the Sikhs' aspiration for autonomy, for right to self-determination at least within the province of Punjab (fondly called Punjabi Suba), which has, for all practical purposes, been denied to them since Independence.

Perspective on Peace

The Sikh commitment to peace has to be judged in the light of tenets and principles put forth in the Guru's teachings, as well as the spirit and orientation of the community's struggle during the five centuries of its history. The concept of peace as freedom from disquieting or oppressive thoughts or emotions appeals to them. They would welcome the definition of 'peace' as "a state in which man is integrated with himself and with his fellows." Because, "judged in this light, peace may be said to be another name for liberation or freedom from human bondage." Surely, "the problem of peace is an exclusive concern of human beings:" the problem does not arise in the case of other creatures, as viewed by Professor N. V. Banerjee.[10] The Sikh teaching accords with the internal and external (i.e. social) dimensions of peace cited in Banerjee's definition. Spiritually, the scriptural word (Gurbani) orients the individual to a blissful state of equipoise. Socially, Sikhism stands for peace and non-voilence, because "no civilized life, including religious, is possible without peace." However, "when all humanly possible peaceful avenues become infructuous and there is danger to one's very existence, recourse to armed resistance is not frowned upon by Sikhism. But that has to be the last resort."[11]

Since the wielding of the sword is warranted in extenuating circumstances, the Sikh faith cannot be labelled 'pacifist' in an absolute sense. Nor is it a cult of war or supporter of militarism. Glorification of war has never been its slogan, even if Sikhism upholds war against evil, oppression and aggression. Once engaged in a battle, the Sikh soldier would fight to the finish, would welcome death rather than defeat or retreat. 'Victory, to be sure' becomes his motto. The symbol of placing one's head over one's palm, implying supreme sacrifice for a noble cause, truly reflects the Sikh spirit and tradition. A factor that strengthens the community's support for peace, is the place of prestige given to women by the Sikh canon and tradition. The women would scarcely opt for war, should the prospect for peace be within the realm of probability.

The sword (as a symbol) stands for 'power', both temporal and spiritual, in Sikhism. The concept was introduced by Guru Hargobind, the sixth Nanak, when he wore two swords, of Miri (temporal power) and

Piri (Spirituality), on his person. The tradition has remained alive up to the present day, when the question of relationship between politics and religion has been hotly discussed in the context of what is known as the Punjab problem.

The present century has been witness to a series of wars besides two World Wars, involving hundreds of thousands of lives lost or crippled. At the same time it has produced a few stalwarts, such as Mahatma Gandhi and Aldous Huxley, who were absolute pacifists, as also a number of others who advocated pacifism of one sort or another (John Dewey, Bertrand Russell, et al). For Gandhi, non-violence is the highest value in life; it satisfies the test of 'universal applicability' and is equated with 'love' which is the very basis of non-violence. However, "when the choice is between violence and cowardice he would support the former." It was much better to defend one's family and property by violence rather than to run away like cowards.[12] It is evident that despite the emphasis on pacifism in Gandhian thought, in essence it upholds the life of courage, Gandhi's ideal man being the 'fearless' one. The Sikh position, though not 'pacifist' in Gandhian sense, subscribes to the virtues of courage and forbearance. Guru Tegh Bahadur's definition of a spiritually awakened person is couched in these terms :[13]

Not to frighten anyone
Nor to be afraid.

The Psalm of Peace

Guru Arjan, the fifth Nanak-Light, bequeathed to his disciples a composition *Sukhmani*, which was rendedred into English by the renowned Sikh savant and aesthete, Professor Teja Singh, under the title 'The Psalm of Peace'. The message of Guru Arjan contained in the text undoubtedly refers to spiritual peace for man. What is true of *Sukhmani*, is also true of the entire scripture. The Guru Granth consists of psalms of peace composed by 36 dedicated souls, under divine inspiration. As Nicholas Roerich, in his Foreword to *The Psalm of Peace*, said in 1937 (before the outbreak of World War II), "this devotional prayer for peace is needed at present more than ever… Where the language of heart speaks, there one can find true enlightenment. …The call for peace and cooperation is indeed a call for creative labour, for Good and Bliss !"[14]

A peaceable mind, trained in the discipline of harmonious relation with oneself and liberated from the shackles of egocentricity, can be depended upon for the maintenance of harmony with fellow beings. The root metaphor of Guru-Granth teaching is *haumai* (egoity) that is to be sublimated and brought under the enlightened discipline of rationality. That is the meaning of freedom from bondgae in Sikhism. The emancipated individual with peace in his/her mind, is capable of aspiring and working for peaceful human relations. Sikhism is one with all those religious faiths of the world that place the comprehensive well-being of humanity in focus. The congregational prayer of the Sikhs concludes with the words: "Let the welfare of all be Thy gracious Will."

Guru Nanak and his nine spiritual successors promoted a specific methodology for the attainment of harmony and peace for their disciples. This was the way of contemplation and love of God, coupled with voluntary service to the needy. A devout Sikh is identified by his contemplative-cum-altruistic conduct of life. Such a dedicated soul would not entertain thoughts of destruction or desire elimination of human life, much less nuclear holocaust. As observed by Sirdar Kapur Singh, "under the impact of world wars, revolutions and dictatorships, we are witnessing a revival of interest in heroes and hero-worship." But all this has "resulted in the modern Fascist and Nazi system of Government." Citing Guru Gobind Singh, he says : "A Sikh must cultivate fortitude and patience and make reason as his guide in all matters. This respect for and reliance on reason, makes the Sikhs peculiarly fit for politico-democratic activities, and renders them sympathetic to the modern democratic tradition."[15] Herein is summed up the Sikh attitude to World Peace.

NOTES

1. From the paper 'Consciousness of Sikh Identity', presented at the Heidelberg University meet and published in the University's Bulletin, 1986 (off-print).
2. Ibid.
3. *Pacnchbati Sandesh*, January 1990, Dehra Dun, India.
4. Harbans Singh, *The Heritage of the Sikhs*, New Delhi : Manohar, 1983, pp.273-4.
5. Ibid., pp.275-6.
6. Ibid., p.267.
7. Gopal Singh, *A History of the Sikh People* 1469-1978, New Delhi : World Sikh Univrsity Press, 1979, pp.650, 662.
8. Rajinder Puri, *Rediscovery of India*, Delhi : SCAN Publishers, 1989. Also excerpted in the Tribune, Chandigarh, April 29, 1989.
9. Ibid.

10. N.V.Banerjee, *Towards Perpetual Peace*, Shimla : Indian Institute of Advanced Study (Delhi : Motilal), 1988, pp. 3-5.
11. Pritam Singh, 'Religion for Peace and Integration', Wazir Singh (Ed.), *Religious Pluralism and Co-existence*, Patiala : Punjabi University, 1986, p.51.
12. Joseph Kuttianical, 'Non-violence the Core of Religous Experience in Gandhi', *Journal of Dharma*, Bangalore, July 1989.
13. Guru Granth Sahib, p.1427.
14. Teja Singh, The *Psalm of Peace*, Amritsar, 1938/1967, Foreword.
15. Kapur Singh, *Parasarprasna*, Jalandhar, 1959 (Amritsar : 1989)pp.42-43, 382.

THE SIKH VIEW OF HUMANISM

The Sikh is committed to Man *and* God. The outlook of the Sikh is marked by inclusivism; both theism and humanism find favour with him. It is not an approach of either this or that, of accepting one at the cost of the other. Faith in God to the exclusion of concern for man has never been the forte of the Sikh. As disciples of the Ten Gurus, the Sikhs have imbibed a spirit of service to humanity as well as contemplation of the Divine. This is borne out not only by the teachings enshrined in the holy Granth, but by the tradition established and followed during the five centuries of Sikhism.

It has been customary with scholars to pose humanism as a system of belief opposed to theistic faith. For them, one could either be a theist or humanist; that is, if one is convinced of the existence of a Divine Power controlling the affairs of the world, one is obliged not to treat man as of primary significane. Those of the thinkers who place man at the centre of the universe, or for whom man is the measure of all things, forfeit the claim to be believers in Godhead, according to this line of thinking. Such a rigid stance pushes the conflict between God-centred and man-oriented ideologies to the extreme, invoking the posture of exclusivism. The question arises: why cannot a humanist believe in God? And what prevents a theist from subscribing to humanism as a philosophy, ideology or faith?

The Sikh Approach to Humanism

Sikhism, as a religion, aims at humanizing man and not dehumanizing him. The essential core of the Gurus' teaching is telling man to be more humane, to be more and more *human.* The philosophy of Sikh religion unfolds the values that inspire its adherents to be guided by the light of reason in their search for perfection. The supreme value termed *Brahman Gyan*, enunciated in *Gurbani*, is verily the vision of the Supreme Reality itself. It affords absolute knowledge to the human seeker, raising him to the level of the Divine. In a sense, it is experience of 'merging' - that of the individual into the ground of his being. The disciple taking to the path indicated by the Gurus, is firmly convinced of the divine nature of his origin. In his endeavour to evolve as a better human being, he is guided at each step by the beatific vision of the seers whose word is enshrined in the *Guru Granth.* His humanistic pursuit is tempered with his theistic make-up.

The Sikh, true to his salt, cannot run away from either theism or humanism. Both are ingrained in his being. To be a Sikh means to have faith in the teachings of the *Guru Granth*, which leaves little scope for rejecting theism. It also means self-transcendence, which implies a progressive inculcation of all-embracing values, that is, intimate involvement in the promotion of human welfare. The Sikh way of life prescribes or at least takes in its stride, an attitude of prayerfulness. The Sikh prayer, addressed as it is to the Supreme Being, affirms the theistic faith of the disciple, on the one hand, and reminds him of his obligation to the community, with its enunciation of the principle of *Sarbat-ka-bhala*, on the other. Evidently, the Sikh approach to humanism combines its value-oriented core with an enlightened faith in the cosmic support to human endeavour.

To say that Guru Nanak and his nine successors were humanists does not mean that they held Man to be primary and the Divine, secondary. In the world view of the Gurus, man is an emanation from the spiritual Essence, and as such cannot claim primacy over his divine source. He, however, is the over-lord of this earth, the rest of the creatures "slaving" for him.[1] All the teachings of the Gurus, all their pious exhortations are addressed to Man; they are meant to raise him to higher and higher levels of perfection. Even the realization of his own divine origin and the re-kindling of faith in the divine dispensation, serve the interest of Man and not of God. In fact, the whole problem of religion is problem of man. God, as the Tenth Guru says, is above all religions.[2] The appeal to God is made for the benefit of man. A divinely oriented soul, a *gurmukh*, is surely a better specimen of humanity, since he is endowed with a willingness to serve human causes. His devotion to God in effect means service to mankind. His theism and his humanism converge to each other, the end-product of this convergence being the merger and identity of the two.

Theistic Humanism of Guru Nanak

That the humanism of Guru nanak is replete with faith, is indisputable. The Guru clearly asserts that his utterings are inspired by the revealed word of his Master.[3] What he utters is for the consumption of men and women of his land, of humanity at large. He shakes the people out of their slumbers of ignorance, superstition and formalism; he makes them aware of the hollowness of casteism, asceticism and renunciation; he warns them against defeatism, hypocrisy and covetousness. On the positive side, Guru Nanak advocates a life that 'wears' the finery inside, even though the coarse outside.[4] Elegance of the heart is preferred to the false elegance of apparel and ostentation. The real worth of the individual is measured in terms of the values he cherishes, the virtues he practises, the duties he performs. One who fails to promote in one's life neither harmony nor wisdom (*naad* and *veda*), develops neither sensibility for music nor aesthetic taste, possesses neither awareness and intellect, nor basic intelligence and secret of the alphabet, – such a one is rated by Guru Nanak as no better than the poor ass.[5] Misplaced pride in one's acquisitions without real virtues, is despised by the Guru in no uncertain terms.

Human salvation is as much a concern of Guru Nanak as of any other sprititual mentor and/or humanist. The way of life recommended by the Guru combines the elements of salvation by faith and knowledge and salvation by divine grace. If we approach his philosophy from the mystical angle, we find him supporting the case of inner illumination, of absolute consciousness or *Brahman-gyan.* If we take into consideration the stress he lays on divine grace, the pathway of devotion and faith, qualifying the individual for the final blessing, would commend itself. Besides, the Guru underlined the indispensability of ethical action as the foundation of spiritual life: "No devotion is complete, without the moral deeds," – says he.[6] At the same time, the blissfull state of aesthetic enjoyment (ecstasy/*vismad*) finds favour with him. Ecstasy comes from the vision of sublimity inside; it also comes from the grandeur of nature outside. The man of action and the man of devotion, the seeker after knowledge and the one resigning himself to the divine will, all have a place in Guru Nanak's scheme of salvation.

The devotional humanism of the *Bhakti* cult popularized belief in meditation, singing the Lord's praises and surrendering onself to Him, constantly looking forward to his act of grace. No doubt, Guru Nanak carries forward the spirit of *bhakti*, but his philosophy focused on the restructuring of human faculties, enabling the individual to meet the challenge of life squarely and face its problems boldly. The epithet of *jodha-mahabali-surma* is one of his favourite expressions, indicating his support for the valiant spirit as well as for a life of vigorous activity. To be born as a human being is a rare privilege, according to Guru Nanak's philosophy. To make the best of this gift of life, physically and mentally, on aesthetic and ethical levels, as also on the spiritual plane, must be one's foremost endeavour. It is to this comprehensive objective that Guru Nanak's theistic humanism is geared. This seems to be the message of his *Namyoga*; this indeed is the spirit of his insistence on Truth and conduct truthful.

Man and Divine

"There is no conflict between religion and a reasonable humanism." This is the view of Dr Radhakrishnan who adds : "When the humanist admits the ultimateness of the values, he is implicitly accepting the spiritual view of the universe."[7] The argument supports the Sikh approach to the humanist ideal, without attempting to make a "religion" of humanism. Dr Radhakrishnan cautions: "Humanism is a legitimate protest against those forms of religion which separate the secular and the sacred, divide time and eternity and break up the unity of soul and flesh." "Every religion should have sufficient respect for the dignity of man and the right of human personality."[8] Indeed, the religion that took its birth with the proclamation of Guru Nanak affirming human dignity, raised a voice of protest against distortions of the human personality brought about by the ruling and priestly vested interests, coupled with the ignorance and passivity of the common man. The protestant character of the Sikh movement is explained by the initiative on Guru Nanak's part, in the socio-secular sphere.

The spiritual dimension of Sikhism has nothing to do with protestantism, except for the solitary note in Guru Nanak's *Babar Vani* where he says : "If the mighty molest the mighty/No feeling of protest rises in my mind/But should a ferocious tiger attack the feeble herd/I would question even my Lord."[9] In the same vein, he addresses the Divine Controller of worldly affairs: "People suffered endless tortures and wailed/Didst Thou have no compassion for them?"[10] Apart from this, the relation between man and God is depicted in the *Guru-Granth* hymns on a purely mystical plane. God is posed as the Spouse and the human soul as the female seeking union with Him. One type of synthesis of the human and the Divine is like a drop merging in the ocean of Eternal Being, losing its finite identity forever. The other type of union is one that is accomplished in the human soul. It is not necessarily the drop that enters the ocean and gets lost in its vastness, but it may be the ocean flowing into the individual stream of consciousness: "The drop is contained in the ocean, the ocean in the drop/Yet, who can understand?-The one who comes to know the secret."[11]

Considered in terms of values, the relation of man and God takes on the form of relationship between essences. The Sikh view of the life conceives the world as filled with Essence; the Divine Spirit informs the entire existence, the pervades all hearts. It explains the origin of man in terms of the "light" that the Absolute is. In other words, the Divine is the Essence of all essences and the Value of all values. The Sikh metaphysics posits the Supreme Reality as "fact" and "value" fused into one. The world is characterized as the abode of Truth; the True One resides therein.[12] To realize the Truth, one has to 'dis-cover' it, to experience it as essence-in-existence, to realize the divine Ordinance (*Hukam*) prevailing all over. This realization is the attainment of the supreme value in Sikhism, variously described as harmony (*abhedata*), absolute consciousness (*Brahman gyan*), salvation-in-life (*jivan mukti*), and state of bliss (*anand*). Such a God–oriented individual (the *Sachiar* or *Gurmukh*) is inwardly in tune with the Infinite, but freely leads the worldly life as a member of the family, as a member of the human community.

The Sikh Spirituality

Spirituality is the quality of spiritual life determined by the elements of belief, values and cultural patterns that are, in turn, influenced by a particular religious tradition or faith. Spiritual quality is the prerogative of the human life. Out of the material and ideal dimensions of one's life, spirituality necessarily belongs to the ideal aspect, even though the material aspect may not be altogether ingnored. The Sikh spiritual life, on this reckoning, is primarily determined by the teaching of *Guru Granth Sahib*, in regard to belief in the Godhead, view of the cosmic existence and human life, nature of salvation and the way of life suited to that goal, as also in regard to the ethical virtues essential for the conduct of social life in terms of the Sikh tradition. The three-fold discipline of earning one's livelihood by honest means *(kirat)*; sharing one's food and possessions with the needy; and meditation by way of *Nam-jaap*, nearly sums up the quality of life prescribed by the Sikh scripture and tradition.

A life of the spirit is not the monopoly of theistic believers or professional spiritualists. It is open even to the non-spiritualist, to the naturalist, to the hardcore humanist. A Buddhist by faith may not subscribe to theism, but may very well say his prayer, meditate on the teachings of Lord Buddha, and lead a life of piety. A philosopher who proclaims to be either a materialist, or naturalist, or non-conformist, and is deeply involved with the question of human values, is certainly not devoid of a life-of-the-spirit. The gnostic individual of Sri Aurobindo's vision is one "whose way of being, thinking, living, acting would be governed by the power of a vast universal spirituality."[13] And, the ideal according to the philosopher Bertrand Russell, is to live in a world without any here-and-now, realizing something of the immensity of our cosmic contemplations. For, the size of man's mind is to be measured by the size and complexity of the universe that he grasps in thought and imagination.[14] The spirit of Sikh spirituality is not far from the vision of these sages and thinkers, with the added emphasis of its firm faith in the unicity of God as expounded in the *Guru Granth*, and recognition of divinity in the humankind.

The Sikh spirituality enjoins upon the adherent to adopt the course of *atam-chinan*, that is, exploration of one's self. For, it is here that the Supreme Being, the Self of all selves, can be discovered and experienced. Moreover, knowing one's self affords an estimation of one's own worth. It leads to a vision of the values that bring fulfilment, not only for the gross and emotive, but for the finer dimensions of life comprising the rational and artistic, the moral and spiritual. It gives the individual a feel of his ultimate concern, something that he prizes most in life, transcending all that is profane and impious. The Sikh spirituality opens up a broad vista of liberation, of emancipation-in-life through the taming of the ego. One who treads the path indicated by the Gurus, gradually sheds his egoism and embraces humanism. Not only does he have vision of the Ultimate, but falls in love with the values that elevate his spirit to even new heights. Such a one realizes that the highest of the high that seemed distant and beyond, veiled and transcendent, is just within reach, fully unveiled and revealed, as if present in the deepest caves of one's heart. The way of *atam-chinan* works up the miracle.

Moral Vision and Virtues

The humanist orientation of Sikhism encompasses the vision of values that constitute the ideal and moral virtues that prepare the individual for enjoying a life of fulfilment. The vices and virtues have not been treated in the scriptural compositions, in the fashion of a philosophical text, nor are they listed under a particular chapter-head. References to the virtues worthy of pursuit in life form part of the spiritual outpourings of the poet-philosphers of *Guru-Granth Bani,* and are found scattered all over the pages of the volume. Some of the major virtues gleaned from the *Bani* are presented here, without attempting a specific hierarchy of the cardinal virtues of Sikhism:

(1) Wisdom. - The Gurus accord a place of honour to thoughtful and rational disposition. The anvil of intellect and apparatus of wise learning are parts of the holy mint.[15] The discipline of reason over the passion-

ridden mind finds a mention in the daily prayer of the Sikhs.[16] Only the awakened soul can ponder the essence.

(2) Contentment — For the excellence of an individual life, the virtue of contentment seems indispensable. Moreover, service as a social act can be performed by the contented souls. One who practises contentment prefers sufferings to a life of dishonour. Says Guru Nanak : If one lives with honour lost/Unworthy is all what he eats.[17]

(3) Truthfulness — All else falls short of Truth, yet higher than truth is conduct truthful.[18] That is the teaching of Guru Nanak who attaches such a high value to purity of conduct, to self-control, to fidelity and chastity.

(4) Non-attachment — The commandment of non-attachment follows the ancient dictum of leading life like a lotus flower that remains dry and detached while floating on the water. Gurbani warns man against indulgence in the gross pleasure of life, but does not preach renunciation or escape as the way out.

(5) Temperance — The control of a well-groomed life-style over the desires, greed and passions of worldly life is recommended in terms of temperance. A stern castigation of life without moderation is available in these words :

Cursed be the life that is led
Only to eat and swell the belly.[19]

(6) Effort — As an ethical virtue, effort (*uddam*) provides the inspiration to accomplish one's tasks through one's own labour. He who exercises the virtue of effort, need not lead a life of dependence. However, *Gurbani* does not advocate a form of effort or activity that leads man to take pride in his own power and to disregard the part played by Divine Grace.

(7) Fearlessness — Ethical theories, both classical and modern, have placed fortitude, valiance or fearlessness among the cardinal virtues. Man, on begetting Truth, sheds all fear. Guru Tegh Bahadur defines a man of wisdom, thus :

Not to frighten anyone, nor to be afraid.[20]

(8) Compassion — According to Guru Arjan, contentment in mind and compassion for all, lead to perfection of the righteous life. The virtue of forgiveness-compassion recommended in the *Bani*, points to the humanist spirit of the teaching. For Sheikh Farid, a *bhakta* is the one imbued with a spirit of sacrifice, one who shares even when dispossessed.[21]

(9) Humility. - The sweet modesty is the hallmark of virtues, according to Guru Nanak who insists that wherever we may be, let us utter decent words. Baba Farid is one with the Guru:

> Utter not words that hurt
> The True Lord resides in all beings.[23]

(10) Aesthetic discrimination. - *Gurbani* commends aesthetic discrimination as a trait of the sensible individual. It inspires the disciples to develop higher tastes and nobler pursuits. Sense for music is one such quality. *Kirtan* is rated as an invaluable gem.[24] And the joy derived from deditation surpasses all joys.

The Sikh ethics with its vision of the spiritual ideal and humanistic orientation, forms a concrete basis for the excellence of the individual and community life. Ethics is not only a key to the spiritual welfare of man, it is a worthy way of life, saturated with the discipline of virtuous acts and the vision of universal human welfare.

NOTES

1. Guru Arjan (Rag Asa), *Guru Granth*, p.374.
2. Jaap, Dasam Granth.
3. Guru nanak (Tilang), *Guru Granth*, p.722.
4. Guru Granth (Var Asa), p.473.
5. Guru Nanak, *Guru Granth*, p.1246; p.1411.
6. Japuji (stanza 21).
7. *An Idealist View of Life*.
8. *The Recovery of Faith*.
9. Guru Granth, p.360.
10. *Iibid.*
11. Guru Nanak, *Guru Granth* (Ramakali), p.878.
12. Guru Angad (Var Asa), *Guru Granth*, p.463.
13. *The Life Divine*.
14. See 'The Expanding Mental Universe' in *Adventures of the Mind*, 1959.
15. *Guru Nanak*, Japuji (stanza 38).
16. Cf. *Ardas*.
17. *Guru Granth* (Var Majh), p.142.
18. *Guri Granth* (Sri Rag), p.62.
19. *Guru Nanak*, *Guru Granth* (Var Suhi), p.790.
20. *Guru Granth*, p.1427, Salokas.
21. *Guru Granth*, Salokas of Sheikh Farid, verse No.128.
22. *Guru Granth*, Var Asa, p.470.
23. *Guru Granth*, Salik Farid (No.129).
24. Guru Arjan, *Guru Granth* (Ramakali), p.893.

THE SIKH APPROACH TO PRAYER

The phenomenon of prayer is grounded in religious faith. This assumption is supported by obervation of the expressions that religious life takes in unfolding itself. When a human individual is engaged in prayer, he or she is performing an essentially religious act, just as a person casting vote in an election is said to perform political act. Manifestations of religious life are numerous; they include worship and sacraments, meditation and trance, rituals and ceremonies, congregation and dissemination of faith, sermons and service, and of course the vaiours forms of prayer. The life of religion may be possible even without an ostensible manifestation; it may consist in a deeply personal experience, popularly known as mysticism, with its attendant state of rapture and ineffability. Even so, it is prayer that is recognized as the essence of religion. The Sikh faith is in complete agreement with this assertion.

The spirit of prayer is indissolubly associated with faith, blind or enlightened. Prayer without faith is no prayer, unless it is only a sham, or pretence, or hypocritical show-off. The faith may be in the Divine, in a prophet, a messenger of God, a spiritual mentor, a scripture, an idol, or any object or power believed to be sanctified and/or supernatural. The object of faith may be one, or a combination of two or more elements, may be a trinity, may be a succession of incarnations. Prayer is believed to bring the subject and the object together, the subject being the person/s in prayer, and the object to whom (or which) the prayer is addressed in a spirit of faith, no matter of what intensity or degree. An individual may 'believe' himself to be an enlightened one, with no faith in the efficacy of a supernatural power etc., yet the same very person may have a deep-seated "faith" underlying his enlightened build-up. Faith does not preclude enlightenment, nor the other way round.

The Paradox of Religion

Prayer necessarily implies dualism of sorts. At the same time it is one of the basic religious categories, and can hardly afford a conflict between itself and some of the other categories of religion. For instance, prayer cannot reject monotheism or, for that matter, any form of theism, including polytheism. It may reconcile itself even with atheism. But, when it comes to absolutism, the religious category of prayer gets involved in conflict with another category, no less religious. The philosopy of absolute idealism posits a single, all-inclusive spiritual reality, which in the religious terminology may be called the Divine, the Universal Being, the Cosmic Spirit, or simply God. The ultimate Reality of philosoply is readily the Supreme Reality of religion.

The Absolute of philosophy leaves no scope for "the other," by definition it cannot. And if the Absolute is equivalent to the absolute Spirit, that is the Divine, all differentiation of subject and object, "I" and "Thou" breaks down. It is all oneness, unicity, or non-duality. Philosophically, it may be characterized as "monism". In such a framework, what could be the status of prayer? For, prayer implies a relation between the subject and the object, between "I" and "Thou". The paradox of religion arises from the acceptance of a monistic metaphysics on the one hand, and a dualistic ontology of prayer on the other. Both absolutism and prayer being basic categories of religion, the problem can neither be resloved nor dissolved in a completely satisfactory manner.

Prayer is essentially a human affair. A human being says his prayer, or engages himself in the act of prayer. Through the activity of prayer, he establishes a relation with the object of prayer, which may be human or non-human in nature. In most cases, the assumption is that a deity or super-human spirit, endowed with the capacity to respond, is present at the receiving end. Man addresses the prayer to It/Him; the object (It/He) "listens to" and understands the prayer so addressed, and decides what to do about it. One of the parties has to be human, whereas the other party in prayer must share the human property of awareness, of understanding, of cognition, as well as the power to respond. A sentient being communicates with another sentient being, of a higher order, perhaps a disembodied spiritual being.

Philosophically, the spiritual being of the highest order is the Supreme Reality or the Absolute itself. All beings, sentient or otherwise, belong to the Absolute, sharing in some degree its spiritual essence. A human being engaged in prayer, on this view, is already related to the absolute Spirit from which he emanates, and seeks the blessing of that Spirit, in addition. The Absolute is at the base, and the Absolute itself is the superlative object of realization for the beings imbued with the impulse to pray. A self-differentiating absolute Spirit seems to have given rise to the subjects, itself remaining the ultimate object, of prayer. The dualistic ontology, requiring a status for man distinct from the entity he prays to, is thus assimilated into the monisitic metaphysics of the Supreme Being endowed with creativity and cognition, cosmic ordinance and graciousness.

The Sikh Prayer

The conceptual framework of Sikhism, more or less, accords with the metaphysical-spiritualistic framework outlined above. The Sikh conception of the Absolute (Brahman) treats it as Impersonal-Personal entity, combining in Itself the dimensions of transcendence and immanence, eternality and temporality, unicity and diversity. The Absolute-cum-God of Sikhism is the Unmanifest-Manifest reality; the Formless, Infinite Being, shining through all the finite forms emanating from It; the pre-Creation Void in the state of trance, creating the world of names and forms at will, and maintaining Essence-in-Existence in the cosmic phase of Self-differentiation. All the "selves" imbibe the Divine selfhood; Man being the pinnacle of all creation stands out of all the species, which only "slave" for him. The spiritual mentors (Gurus) of Sikhism enjoin upon Man to discover and recognize his spiritual base and essence.

A Sikh (disciple/follower) of the Gurus is supposed to engage himself/herself in prayer in all situations of life. "Prayer" does not mean the formal mode of prayer in all cases. Emphasis is placed on faith and sense of humility with which the prayer is offered. It is addressed to the personal, omniscient, gracious aspect of the Divine who is believed to share the emotions of the human world. A disciple may choose to say his prayer to one (or more) of the Gurus believed to have embodied the spirit Divine. The essence of Sikh prayer is the one-to-one relation of communion between man and God. The motivation for prayer may come from any situation of life, be it a need for material gain, be it the safety and security of oneself and companions, for peace of mind, for health and happiness, for thanksgiving, for spiritual progress, for a life attuned to the Divine. In situations of distress and grief, the prayer might be a petition for solace and comfort, for consolation and for courage-to-be.

The psychology of prayer unmistakably points to the morale-boosting effect of prayer on the subject concerned. Sikhism indeed recognizes this significant aspect of prayer, in recommending that the disciple seek a constant state of "ascendance" - abiding in "high spirits" even in adverse circumstances. However, the philosophy of Sikh prayer goes a step further than the psychology of keeping the morale high. The ultimate of Sikh prayer is an attitude of life; a life-style imbued with faith. The discipline of the Sikh prepares him for the performing of his daily chores and duties with prayerfulness in the mind. In a sense, the entire text of the Guru Granth is prayer. Its reading and recitation is but an act of prayer on the part of the disciple.

Articulation is just one mode of prayer, – and perhaps a necessary and most widely adopted mode. But, a silent, speechless prayer that characterizes the life-attitude of a devotee, without the need of words, can be "said" through feelings. The attitude of faith, in prayer, integrates the human faculites, with intellect acting in harmony with the emotion. If at all there is seeking in such prayerful attitude, it is illustrated in Guru Arjan's expression:

> I seek not power and pelf,
> I seek not salvation either;
> In my mind, what I beseech
> is the love of Thy noble feet.

The disciple of the Guru, in such an exalted state of the spirit, is not concerned whether his prayers are answered or not. For him, it is to pray, and not to expect results, or rewards.

A philosophy like Naturalism inspires little belief or faith in prayer and its efficacy. According to its doctrine nature does what it does, irrespective of the wishes, desires or prayers of human beings; no amount of prayer would alter the course of events in the order of nature. But, Sikhism does not subscribe to such naturalistic framework. The Sikh spirituality inculcates the faith that God is influenced by his loving devotees, in as much as the parent is moved by the entreaties of the children. A hymn of Guru Arjan (in translation) reads as follows:

> (You are really a hard nut to crack!)
> Whatever effort may we make, You are not pleased.
> You are not won over, whatever scriptures may we read.
> You are not controlled, through ablutions at holy spots,
> You are not conquered, through conquest of the Globe.
> Not through feats intellectual, are you caressed,
> Not through bountiful charities, are You impressed.
> You control all, O infinite transcendent Lord,
> The devotees alone control You –
> with power that You afford.
>
> (Guru Granth, p.962)

The Formal Mode of Prayer

Sikhism prescribes no posture, ritual or situation for the expression of prayer. Any place, any mood is fit for it. No hour is fixed for prayer: all time is time for prayer. But, this is in regard to the individual's interior, personal communication with the Spirit divine. The Sikh tradition has evolved another, typically formal, mode of prayer too. This mode takes on the form of corporate prayer that is offered ceremonially on special occasions of the day, or month, or year. The wording of this "formal" prayer is not completely fixed: new lines have been added to its text several times over the course of decades. Its length too has varied; flexibility is permitted to suit the given occasion and mood of the congregation. The part that does not change, however, is the opening stanza and the final verse. The characteristic mark of the formal Sikh prayer is the entire assembly standing with folded hands, facing the scripture, and one member leading the prayer in loud tones. This duty to lead the prayer may be delegated to any worthy Sikh, not necessarily a priest by profession.

The formal mode of prayer may be employed even by a solitary believer, at the end of his morning/evening routine discipline of reciting the hymns. He may stand up, as if in front of the the Guru Granth, and lead the *Ardasa* (formal prayer) for himself. Normally, however, this mode is adopted as a mass in the Sikh temple, i.e. Gur-Dwara (lit. the abode of God/Guru), where the followers assemble in congregation. Most of the devout families keep a room in the house reserved for the holy *Guru Granth*, make ceremonial obeisance before it, and offer their formal prayer collectively or individually, as the situation may be.

The formal prayer starts with an invocation to the Almighty symbolized by the "sword" representing "power". The stanza is taken from the *Dasam-Granth* text bearing the title "Ode to Durga." The original stanza invokes the blessings of, besides the omnipotent Divine, nine of the Gurus; the Sikh tradition has added the name of the Tenth Master and Guru Granth, as a supplement. The second part of the prayer reminds the congregation of the holy spots and places of worship, besides personages from the Sikh history, who made supreme sacrifies, embraced martyrdom, leading struggles against unjust rulers and enemies of the Sikhs. This is the part that is flexible enough to accommodate references to newer events.

The third part of the formal prayer is offered in the name of the entire Sikh community, seeking the gift of holy Name, i.e. contemplation of the Lord, his protection, his blessing. Some of the phrases employed in this part afford rare insights into the cultural pattern of the Sikhs. For instance, reference to "Deg, Tegh, Fateh" speaks of "cooking" (economic aspect), "sword" (fighting spirit) and "victory" (high morale). Similarly, reference to "passions in check" and "reason in ascendance" alludes to the need of a balanced life. Then follows the fourth part, wherein mention is made of the special occasion for the prayer, may be an event of joy, may be the last rites of a dead one, or may be the conclusion of a session of *Gurbani* recitation. Mention is also made of the special offerings, if any, in the form of cash, drapings, *prasad* (the sweet flour-pudding distributed among the members of the congregation), and so on.

The final touch is given with the short verse which (in translation) reads:

Nanak seeks the boon of
Thy Name and spirits high;
In Thy will, grant
the good of all mankind!

That is the ending of the prayer, the fifth part, beseeching the well-being of the entire human race.

As a document of invocation, homage, and spirit of humility, coupled with thanksgiving and humanistic intent, the formal Sikh Prayer is nothing less than a paradigm of religio-cultural orientation of a community. Its presupposition of the basic unity of mankind can be appreciated from its articulation of the supreme value in terms of "universal welfare", without distinctions of caste, class, colour or country. The Gandhian formulation of "Sarvodaya" (lit. the uplift of one and all) is perhaps the nearest approach to the cosmopolitan intent of the Sikh prayer. With the inmost, personal, existential core of prayerfulness at one pole, and the open-ended, corporate prayer at the other pole, Sikhism places before humanity Guru Nanak's message of love, of piety, of voluntary service. For the Sikh, the act of prayer is its own fulfilment.

THE SIKH VIEW OF SALVATION

The expression *jivan mukti*, the Sikh ideal of salvation, is composed of two components, 'jivan' (life) and 'mukti' (emancipation), implying emancipation-in-life. The term though rooted in the classical Indian traditon, finds its fullest expression in the sixteenth-century compositions of the *Adi-Granth.* It refers to the highest spiritual state of the individual, in tune with the Ultimate and at peace with human society. One who attains to the exalted state of liberation during one's lifetime, is called *Jivan Mukta*, the emancipated-in-life. The attributes of such a living being are mentioned by the Gurus at numerous places in their Bani (compositions, hymns).

The ideal of human life in terms of Sikh spirituality is variously characterized as harmony (*abhedata*), blissfulness (*anand*), Divine consciousness or enlightenment (*Brahman-gyan*), as also *jivan mukti.* The latter is encompassed by the more comprehensive conception of Salvation encountered in practically all the religious faiths. In the extended sense, salvation goes beyond its religious meaning; someone may have his salvation in the acquisition of wealth, that is, something which protects him against poverty and insecurity. But it is the spiritual meaning of salvation that goes into the doctrinal study, viz. soteriology. The Indian figures of *moksha, mukti, nirvana,* as well as several of their equivalents employed in the *Adi Granth* (e.g. *param pad, nirban pad*) are covered under the soteriological study of the theories of spiritual emancipation.

The most common conception of salvation in the Indian context, denotes 'deliverance' of the human soul from the cycle of rebirths. Human life is involved in suffering (*dukkha*) and the final salvation of man, especially in Buddhistic terms, is escape from *dukkha*, which becomes possible with the end of earthly life, either in the form of renunciation or in *nirvana.* Mukti as liberation also implies freedom from bondage which comes with the cessation of transmigration process. When a being is no longer alive, and no longer taking births, that being is liberated both from suffering and from bondage. "The final aim of a human being, as put by P. L. Bhargava, "is to attain salvation which leads to the cessation of birth and death and the enjoyment of eternal bliss." According to the Hindu view, "with spiritual knowledge, disinterested service and devotion to God one becomes qualified to attain salvation.''[1] The question is whether Sikhism subscribes to such a conception of *mukti*, attainable in after-life.

In the continuing tradition of Indian religious thought, belief in *mukti*, as deliverance from the incarnation cycle, keeps recurring, with varying emphases on *karma* and knowledge, grace and bliss, faith as well as other concomitants. The Bhakti cult and Sant poetic tradition freely employed the vocabulary of *mukti*. Similarly, Guru Nanak and his spiritual successors accepted the terminology made current by the preceding generations of sages and men of piety. But, as in the case of numerous other concepts, e.g. the four *yugas*, eighty-four lakhs of species, the trinity of Brahma-Vishnu-Mahesh, *maya* and *sunya*, the expression *mukti* is invested with new meaning in the Bani. Guru Arjan goes to the extent of rejecting *mukti* in the traditional sense, substituting it with constant love of the Divine, as the ideal state of being. It is not the annihilation of human existence that serves as crux in the Sikh conception of *mukti*, but it is the spiritual quality of one's being, instead.

The root-metaphor of Vedantic soteriology is *avidya* (lit. ignorance), and that of Buddhism, *trishna* (lit. craving) leading to suffering. With Guru Nanak, the root-metaphor changed into *haumai* (the individuating sense of ego, or I-am-ness). The Guru treats of 'haumai' as *the* cause of ignorance, craving and bondage, as also of suffering. If emancipation is sought, it is from the shackles of ego. Guru Nanak's definition of *jivan-mukta*, therefore, is in terms of the negation of egoity:

> He alone is emancipated-in-life
> Who is rid of ego inside.
>
> (A.G. p. 1010)

The state of egolessness is the state of perfect detachment, bringing the seeker closest to divinity. The 'gnostic' individual of Aurobindo Ghose's conception is none other than the *jivan-mukta*, to whom are revealed all secrets of being and becoming.[2] He is the one characterized as Brahman-gyani in the Bani, and Boddisattva in Buddhism.

The *jivan-mukta* of Sikh conception is the realized soul, identified as Gurmukh (the God-oriented one). He leads the life of a common householder, enriched with the experience of spiritual harmony within. The Gurmukh is said by the Guru to 'come' and 'go' freely; he moves from one realm to the other, from the worldly involvements to purely spiritual bliss, with little hesitation or hindrance. Guru Arjan emphatically speaks of such a liberated one as attained to *Nirvana-within-grihstha* (family life). The paradoxical expression of dying while alive, is employed by the Gurus in order to stress the importance of abandoning one type of life and the adoption of another, higher type. It is "dying out" of the life of *haumai*, of 'five evils', and entering into the phase of contemplation, altruism and love of God. The person attaining to the state of *jivat-marna* in this sense, is the one qualified for the designation of *jivan-mukta.* He or she is the one to have *dis*-covered the essence of human life, the essential life, concealed under the sheaths of egoism, of ignorance, of passions, of avarice, pride and infatuation. The Gurus in their teachings indicate the path leading to liberation, to emancipation-in-life.

The ideal state of *jivan-mukta* is, notionally, within the reach of every human being, since anyone following the ethico-spiritual course honestly and faithfully, may receive the blessing. Yet, as the Gurus point out, rare are the individuals who actually arrive at the summit. The blessed ones, fortified with the experience of supreme realization, set out to serve their companions. They strive for the total well-being of fellow citizens, in all spheres of human existence. However, the success of a *jivan-mukta* in heralding an order of gnostic individuals or the Kingdom of God on earth, is not to be measured in terms of the number of "converts" to his way of life, but in the spirit of his message coupled with the model of humane, illumined life he presents for emulation.

The emancipated souls in human form are to be found in the Sikh community and outside its fold, only the eye to behold them and discern their merit may be wanting. Discussing 'grace' from the perspective of Christianity, John B. Chethimattam remarks:[3] "Supernatural life according to Christian tradition is an elevation of man beyond the human limits so that he is enabled to share in the life of God himself without losing his human identity and personality." This nearly sums up the quality of *jivan-mukta* in the Sikh tradition.

NOTES

1. P.L. Bhargava, *Fundamentals of Hinduism*, 1982.
2. Cf. Wazir Singh, *Humanism of Guru Nanak*, 1977.
3. *Journal of Dharma* (Bangalore), October-December, 1987.

THE SIKH RESPONSE TO SOCIAL REALITY

Sikhism is a changing tradition. It has been so since its origin five centuries back. Guru Nanak, the first spiritual preceptor of the Sikh faith, was born A.D. 1469, and the first proclamation of the faith came during the first decade of the sixteenth century. One of the primary and potent motivating factors that led to the proclamation of the new faith, was Guru Nanak's concern for social transformation. If contemplation (*simran*) is the inner, intimate aspect of Sikh spirituality, service of love (*seva*) is its social dimension. The culmination of Sikh style of life expresses itself in the formula: Meditate on the Divine Presence; Earn your livelihood through honest labour; Share your earnings and food with others.

Guru Nanak and his nine spiritual successors together make up the galaxy of Ten Masters, the last mentor being Guru Gobind Singh. The Gurus not only bequeathed to their followers a holy book, the *Guru Granth*, but also led the community through struggles against unjust social order and tyrannical rulers, and through crusades against superstition, conventionalism, formalism and decadent priesthood. The life-story of the Gurus is the story of sacrifice and martyrdom. The eventful history of the Sikh community of the entire eighteenth century, following the death of Guru Gobind Singh in 1708, is the history of relentless fight against a host of invaders and marauders; it is a glorious record of persecution and crucifixions suffered at the hands of a withering feudal empire; it is an enthralling tale of the steadfast dedication to the ideals of Truth, well-being of humanity, and life led with honour, inculcated by the Gurus.

The Social Code

An early eighteenth-century document, believed to be the work of a close associate and contemporary of Guru Gobind Singh, lays down the doctrinal bases and principles of corporate living and state polity for the Sikh community. The gist of some of the important passages from the treatise (known as *Prem Sumarag*) is rendered by Professor J. S. Grewal in the following terms:[1]

"Whosoever will follow the code instituted by Guru Gobind Singh would not only save himself but become the agent of liberation for his associates in this world." "The essence of the Sikh way of life could not be reduced to formal observances. A Sikh should be a proof against sensual temptation and indulgence... The watchwords of a Sikh sould be continence, truth, contentment, mercy, duty, humility and service. He should not live on charity; he must earn his own livelihood through honest means." "For a Sikh the communal brotherhood was more important than the ties of kinship. A Sikh should always be ready to share his food, clothes and other belongings with the needy; and if he were in a position to be of any service to others, he should jump at the opportunity regarding it as a mark of God's grace."

"A most important aspect of the government of the Sikh state was the administration·of justice." "Indeed, the *raison d'etre* of the Sikh state was justice. The ruler should remember that power was granted to him for the administation of justice. In life hereafter in the court of the True King he would not be questioned about his devotion to God; but he would be asked how many under his rule had received comfort and how many had suffered misery. He would be held responsible for nothing else but justice in a very comprehensive sense."

"In a limited sense, the ideal Sikh state was to be a welfare state." The ruler "should take care that none in his kingdom was without food, dress or occupation. He should aid every indigent parent to enable him to give his daughter in marriage. In fact, he should fulfil every kind of want, particularly that of a householder. The ruler as a guardian of his subjects should constantly look after the welfare of his subjects."

''The *Khalsa Panth*, though a casteless society, had a social stratification of its own which was based on the difference in economic advantage.''

"Thinking primarily in religious terms, the author insists on equality among the Khalsa who were to form a casteless cociety. This ideal of equality could lead perhaps to social mobility. But the author does not visualize an egalitarian society. In fact, a built-in social stratification based on the difference in economic advantage is already there in this presentation of the Sikh social order."

Sikh Institutions

Much earlier than the compositon of *Prem Sumarag*, Guru Nanak, the founder of Sikh faith, had initiated his followers into organizing themselves as a well-knit community of householders, liberated from religious fanaticism fostered by orthodoxy, developing its own spiritual tradition, and experimenting with its own modes of community life. By the time of Guru Amar Das, third in the spiritual ministry of Guru Nanak, the Sikh institutions had been firmly established. The formost was the institution of Guruship itself. The second was *langar* or the community kitchen serviced by the Guru's disciples for the benefit of visitiors and inmates alike, without distinction of caste, class or status. Another was *sangat* or congregation of the Guru's followers sitting in audience and singing hymns with the accompaniment of music. Still another was the system of rendering relief to people in distress and need, sheltering them and feeding them irrespective of their religious affiliations. The Gurudwara (literally, the abode of Guru) came to be the focal point of all public activities of the Sikhs, besides serving as a centre for imparting spiritual enlightenment.

The Sikh institution of community kitchen is quite well known not only to the people of Punjab and India but to the members of international community who have ever cared to visit a Sikh *gurudwara* in India or abroad. Not only that the food is served to whosoever joins the *pangat* at the mealtime, without obligation whatever, but in most cases shelter is provided to the needy and to those in distress, without asking to which religion they owe allegiance. A *gurudwara* is the abode of God, and therefore the abode of man.

Recounting some of the unorthodox steps that the founders of Sikh faith took to smash the religion-backed, birth-based system of segregation and to make social integration a part of Sikh religious ethos, Professor Pritam Singh refers to the injunction of the Tenth Guru at the Amrit ceremony, to the effect that the initiates into the Khalsa order "have to forget all about their obligations to their previous castes, high or low. They sip the steel-stirred and chant-charged water from the same bowl."[2]

The ideal man of the Sikh conception is characterized in the motto of 'Sant-Sipahi' – the saint-soldier. He is a man of piety with saintly disposition in his ordinary business of life, inwardly absorbed in prayer and contemplation. In the face of challenge, however, he is a fighter par excellence, with high morale and proven valour. He is trained in the art of keeping a balance between a mystic's life and that of a warrior, an equilibrium of idealism and pragmatic orientation.

The Scriptural Base

The holy book of the Sikhs, the *Guru Granth*, apart from its status as a scripture, is a unique literary marvel of the medieval India. It combines in its 1430 large-size pages, 36 poet-philosophers and men of piety drawn from the various regions and communities of the country, presenting a synthesis of their wisdom in a neatly laid-out pattern. Not only that the

Granth is a paradigm of integration in its scheme - a product of Guru Arjan's editorial acumen, the whole orientation ot the holy book is towards 'harmony' of the loftiest order. It is harmony of the individual soul with the ground of its being; a merging of the drop, as it were, with the ocean; or perhaps the flowing of the ocean through the tiny drop. Either way, it is integration of the two entities, leading to spiritual oneness of the human and the divine. Placing in an ascending order the five most outstanding values gleaned from the treasure that is Guru Granth, we obtain the following hierarchy :

(1) Enlightenment, as the basic value, at the level of intellect;
(2) Love, as the humanistic value;
(3) Bliss or *Anand*, the aesthetic value;
(4) Absolute consciousness or *Brahman-gyan*, the cosmic value;
(5) Harmony, value of the spiritual order.

The *yogis* symbolize harmony, or communion, or the mystic union, as realization of *Anhad-Naad* through the 'tenth door'(*Dasam Duar*). The Adviatic thinkers describe it in terms of non-dualism. The Guru Granth Bani employs the epithets of *sabad, naad, abhedata, et al,* to designate the state of harmonious relation between man and God. Evidently, the spirit of harmony permeates the philosophic outlook of the Sikh who assimilates the Guru's teaching. And the whole thrust of the value-system just outlined is well-being of humanity (*sarbatt ka bhala*), without distinctions of caste and class, community and country.

Practically all monotheistic religions subscribe to the belief in the common fatherhood of God and brotherhood of man. Guru Nanak stated this view in un-ambiguous and eloquent terms : "We have one single Divine-Father; all of us are His children."[3] This doctrine of the Divine paternity and human fraternity takes expression in the Guru-Granth compositions in several forms. For instance, "None is my enemy, none alien to me; I am held in friendly bond with all."[4] And in Kabir — "The whole mankind has emerged out of one single Light; why rate some as good and others bad?"[5] The poet-philosophers of the Guru Granth exhorted man, as man, to transcend the demarcations fostered by creed and cult, declaring oneself to be neither a Hindu nor a Musalman. But, keeping in view the social reality, they demanded of both Hindus and Muslims to be good Hindus and good Musalmans, in accordance with their respective spiritual and ethical codes. It is an interesting feature of Guru-Nanak *Bani* that it defines the virtues and qualities of a *yogi* and a *sanyasi,* Musalman and a Hindu, in the true sense of the term.

The Integrative Impulse

The Gurus' response to the national and political situation of their times was not one of un-concern and detached aloofness. In the face of Mughal invasion of India, Guru Nanak talks in terms of *Hindustan*, as his country, threatened by ruthless alien armies. It is rightly said that "of all the medieval poets, it is he who takes the contemporary Pathan rulers to task for having lost the 'gem' of a land, that is India, to Babur, ''who came as the head of a party of sin from Kabul to secure the hand of the bride (India) by force."[6] .In the sixteenth-century perspective, the Pathan rulers, Muslim by faith, were Indian, whereas the Mughal army-men led by Babur, again Muslim, were non-Indian, and hence deserved reproach and resistance, in the eyes of the Guru.

"The Sikh scripture may be the only sacred book of a major religion of the world in which integrative impulse has gone to the extent of incorporating the devotional works of the writers of religions other than its own."[7] Every time a Sikh bows his head before the Holy Book, he bows it not only before the word of his Gurus, but, also before the compositions of Farid and Kabir, Namdev and Ravidas, Dhanna and Sadhna, and a number of other saints and Bhatts - not all of them belonging to the then high castes of Hindus, but also to Muslim/Sufi denominations, weavers, calico-printers, cobblers, butchers, farmers, etc., by caste and vocation.

"Developing an attitude of respectful accommodation towards other religions may be very helpful to the principle of integration, but laying one's own life for the worshipping rights of a religion other than one's own, belongs to the category of a much higher plane of altruism, and this is what Guru Tegh Bahadur, the ninth Guru, did in 1675 in Delhi."[8] The historian A.C. Banerjee pays fulsome tribute to the Guru for this supreme sacrifice, although "protection of *tilak* and *janju* was no part of the Sikh creed."[9] The Sikh shrines, including the Golden Temple at Amritsar, have four doors opening in all the four directions, symbolizing welcome to members of all the four *varnas* of the traditional Indian society, as against the practice of debarring the so-called low-caste persons from entering the precincts of a sacred place of worship.

Humanism of the Sikh

Fortified with the virtues and values inculcated by scriptural teaching and historical setting, the Sikh society has developed a broad, humanistic outlook on matters national and international. The Sikhs may be seen as "deeply involved in the process of differentiation and yet so intent on preserving the principles of integration."[10] To meet the contemporary challenges of widespread loneliness and alienation of man and the increasing sense of meaninglessness of his existence, the disciples of Guru Nanak seek authentic selfhood in their personal encounter with the Formless who shines through all forms, as also in their social commitment, acting upon the message of the Guru that taught : "the essence of learning (*vidya*) is altruism (*par-upkar*)."[11] The set of values that the Sikh community keeps before itself as the ideal to be progessively realized, works out to a scheme for personal as well as collective emancipation. The words of Dr Radhakrishnan aptly sum up the position of Guru Nanak's disciple : "The two elements of selfhood, uniqueness (eachness) and universality (allness) grow together until at last the most unique becomes the most universal."[12] The Sikh operates at a level where his individual salvation is no longer distinguished from human salvation.

Left to himself, undisturbed by parochial considerations, a Sikh is a forward-looking person, with a liberal outlook, brought up in the tradition of *simran* and *seva*, kirat (honest labour) and sharing, and praying for the social-spiritual welfare of mankind. The patriotic sentiment of the Sikh is not debased by a narrow, irrational nationalism, engaged in cut-throat competition that encourages hatred of other peoples and despises alien cultures, but is rooted in genuine love of the motherland, a balanced awareness of its situation and needs, and spirit of responsible endeavour to serve its causes. The Sikh response to social reality is marked by a measure of transcendence. Basically a house-holder, the Sikh would rise above the family ties and infatuations at the call of his community and nation A happy blend of tradition and modernity, with boundless love of the Punjab and India, the greatest moments of inspiration of the Sikh are when he is moved by humanistic and cosmopolitan considerations. His internationalism thrives on a sound nationalism; he believes that one who loves not one's own people, can scarcely love the neighbours and humanity at large. The integrative impulse of the Sikh unites him in harmonious relation with his fellow Punjabis, with his countrymen, and with *homosapiens,* that is, one single human race

Dspiciting the Sikh character in his study on the Sikhs in California, Dr C.H. Loehlin asserts : "The Sikhs have long been noted for their power to adapt themselves to circumstances they cannot control. Their practical optimism and freedom from apathy has led them to accept whatever befalls in the Providence of God and try to turn it to their own advantage." "The Sikhs are traditionally a devout people. Their religion encourages worldly success and social responsibility, values which have obviously helped their progress." The people of Stockton noticing their spirit of service recorded : "Charity was practised by the members and no man applying for shelter or food was ever turned away, regardless of who he was."[13]

Not that all the Sikhs conform to the ideal. Nor is it claimed that caste names and social stratification have completely disappeared from their lives. But essentially, a Sikh is endowed with a liberal outlook and is blessed with a liberated spirit.

NOTES

1. J.S. Grewal, 'The Prem Sumarag : A Theory of Sikh Social Order' in Harbans Singh & Barrier (Ed.), *Essays in Honour of Dr Ganda Singh,* Patiala, 1976, pp. 168-173.
2. Pritam Singh (unpublished papers).
3. *The Guru Granth* (M. 5, Sorath), p. 611.
4. *Ibid.* (M. 5, Kanra), p. 1299.
5. *Ibid.* (Kabir, Prabhati), p. 1349.
6. Pritam Singh (unpublished papers).
7. *Ibid.*
8. *Ibid.*
9. A.C. Banerjee, 'Aurangzeb and the Sikh Gurus' in *Essays in Honour of Dr Ganda Singh (op. cit.),* p. 139.
10. Cf. Martin Buber (quoted by Robert F. Davidson, *Philosophies Men Live By,* 1974).
11. Wazir Singh, *Humanism of Guru Nanak,* Delhi, 1977, p. 184.
12. *Ibid.* (quoted from *An Idealist View of Life*).
13. C.H. Loehlin, 'The Sikhs in California' in *Essays in Honour of Dr Ganda Singh (op. cit.),* p. 297.

DEATH AND SUFFERING IN SIKHISM

Pleasure and Pain are a set of robes
That men must keep on wearing.

- Guru Nanak[1]

Sikhism is not a philosophy of suffering. Even so, human suffering and death are the two running themes in the Sikh poetic tradition. The poet philosophers of *Guru Granth,* the holy scripture, and practically all the commentators and interpreters of the Sikh faith, repeatedly stress these twin facts of human life, not for highlighting them, but to encourage men to face them and to conquer them.

Apart from the ten spiritual mentors (Gurus) of the Sikh religion, six of whom composed hymns incorporated in the *Granth*, Sikhism recognizes a galaxy of medieval saints and divines, thirty-six in number and all poets, equal in rank and reverence for their moral and spiritual teaching. The main thrust of the voluminous compositions of these spiritual luminaries, is to awaken in man the urge to transcend his mundane existence, to inculcate in him love for the aesthetico-spiritual realm of life, to persuade him to imbibe virtues that help in the moulding of a more humane order. All their teaching is addressed to man, for the well-being of man, at the various levels of his existence, – material and mental, aesthetic and ethical, social and spiritual. Their vision keeps in focus the regenerate man, transformed from the ordinary, existential plane of living into a qualitatively higher order of being. The essential man of their vision is one endowed with insight into life itself. Guru Nanak, the first of the Ten Gurus, depicts the existential man covering four periods or 'quarters' of life, from infancy with its ingrained attachement for parents, through youth with its passions, and middle age with its engrossments, leading to the period of decline and the time to depart. In this situation, man keeps on changing into the apparels of pain and pleasure, suffering and joy, with fear of death constantly lurking deep in his being.

Human life may be portrayed in its four periods or ten stages, as found in the compositions of the Gurus and Bhaktas. But that is not the end of the matter. Some of the most forceful utterances, for instance in the hymns of Kabir, are those in which "men are urged to settle their accounts with God before death overtakes them and it is too late." Karine Schomer, illustrating this point with the help of Kabir's couplets, adds: "This theme or urgency in the face of death" is the persistent refrain in Kabir's hymns.[2] And, for that matter, in the *bani* of all the authors of the *Guru Granth.*

Guru Arjan, the fifth Guru and first editor of the *Granth*, chastises man, first of all, to accord welcome to death, giving up all expectation of life; let him be at the service of all, then alone would he countenance God.[3] As for the formula of overcoming anguish and suffering in life, the teaching may be summed up in Guru Arjan's proposition:

> Let my mind bank upon the support of that Lord
> Contemplating whom joy descends and all sufferings vanish.[4]

Theme of Suffering in Gurbani

It is not without interest to note that suffering in all its dimensions, is considered in *Gurbani*, which in this context includes Bhakta-*Bani* as well. Guru Nanak, in *Var-Malar* refers to the "kind of suffering that results from separation, another kind that is caused by hunger, and third type resulting from the unfailing advent of the messenger of death."[5]

However, suffering at the organic level constitutes its physical dimension, depicted in terms of disease and pain, frailties and helplessness effected by intemperate living and/or old age, besides the tortures brought about by sadistic acts. The emotive dimension covers anxieties and pangs of separation, the *birha*, and the seemingly endless wait for re-union. Both the physical and emotive aspects of suffering are also available, where the poetic sensibilities raise a voice of protest against human folly, social inequity and persecution, and even divine indifference. The fourth and fifth dimensions cover existential and spiritual suffering, respectively.

To be human is to suffer: that is the essence of existential suffering, in itself inescapable, but unlike physical pain or grief in its nature. It need not depend upon apprehension of a tragic situation or awareness of an impending calamity or fear. The uncaused anxiety, of which Heidegger speaks, and the existential anguish, of which Sartre speaks, are forms of suffering synonymous with existence itself. Kierkegaard regards such universal suffering as resulting from dread and the perilous tension between time and eternity. According to him, earthly existence is a mysterious blend of anguish and lovely dreams, of creation and despair.[6] The problem of suffering, in this case, is intimately linked with human bondage. Professor Talib uses the phrase 'metaphysical suffering of sheer existence'– to describe the kind of suffering afflicting man who is born in pain and in pain shall he die.[7]

The problem of existential suffering was succintly brought to the fore, perhaps for the first time, by Buddhism, which proclaimed that all is suffering - '*sarvam duhkham*'. But Buddhist philosophy did not make suffering an inalienable feature of human existence. One of its four basic truths was made out to be *nirodhasatya* (the cessation of suffering), *duhkhasatya* (the truth of human misery) not being the sole or absolute truth. "*Nirvana* is the end of suffering, the extinction of desire, the destruction of greed, hate, delusion, and of the constituent factors (*skandhas*) and the volitional forces (*samskaras*)."[8] According to the general rut of Indian systems, "the human individual suffers or enjoys by virtue of his participation in the rolling process (i.e. *samsara*), on account of his sense of identification with it. This is some kind of an 'original sin' which he calls his life or living.''[9] However, the utilitarian orientation of Buddhism coloured most of the subsequent philosophical systems in India. The various prescriptions were held out in accordance with the terms of diagnosis in each case. If craving or *trishna* is the cause of all suffering, then the whole effort should be to root out this 'evil'. If the individuating principle of ego is guilty, then, as in the case of *Gurbani*, utmost emphasis would have to be placed on the taming of egoism. ''The ultimate Truth is not realized in the placing of one's self in the fore,'' says Guru Nanak. ''The summum bonum comes within reach when the sense of ego is banished.''[10]

Guru Nanak's oft-quoted line *Nanak dukhiya subh sansar,* is matched in its sweep by Sheikh Farid's saying: ''I thought I alone suffered, but oh! the whole world is overtaken by grief. From the house-top, each abode is seen equally afire.''[11] A major strand in Farid is existential anguish, illustrated in his couplet that speaks of the midwife snipping the umbilical cord at birth: Better, if she would also press a little the throat; one would not have to face the affairs of life and to bear its sorrows.[12] In point of fact, the root-metaphor of Farid-*Bani* is *Dukh.* The individual, finding himself a solitary, friendless creature in a hostile world, undergoes the experience of anguish to which he is condemned. The spectre of old age haunts him; death holds a siege around him. Poor man! He would be reduced to ashes in the end.[13]

But, the Sikh poetic tradition makes reference to the brighter aspect of *dukh* too. Guru Nanak's phrase ''*Dukh daru, sukh rog*'' alludes to a kind of 'pain' that serves as remedy and 'pleasure' that is the malady. In what sense *sukh* is the root of evil, and suffering welcome for the sake of moral health? An answer is provided by Kierkegaard: ''The suffering which restores man to awareness of sin is also a means to reconciliation, only, however, if one dutifully accepts the suffering and turns it to good purpose.''[14] Suffering is not, in all cases, a misfortune or curse. The thorn in the flesh may be a blessing if it helps one to turn in into a spiritual medicine. That is the creative approach to *dukh*.[15] Granted that suffering is a fundamental factor in the human situation, that it is innate to man, yet the self-inflicted suffering undergone for spiritual purification belongs to another category. Similarly, when man undergoes sorrow that lies in alienation from God, it is not simply on the mundane or profane level that he suffers. His suffering may be productive of moral and spiritual goods; as "Jesus suffered in the cause of God, and through his suffering was said to redeem mankind, from sin and spiritual suffering."[16]

The inscrutable mystery by which the Divine apportions *dukh* and *sukh* to his creatures, finds eloquent expression in Guru Nanak's *Japuji*:

> Countless stand condemned
> to pain and miseries ever:
> Such blessing in disguise
> The Bounteous One may shower.[17]

Here, even the torments are treated as the Lord's gifts. Karl Jaspers' paradox lends support to the view of man taking the 'risk' of being happy: "When a man is unhappy, being himself will be easier than when he is happy."[18] Man is made aware of himself by his suffering, – that seems to be the moral. And the pangs of separation suffered by the soul, are not extolled by Sheikh Farid without reason:

> The pain of *birha* is belittled
> but, *birha*, thou art sovereign!
> A body that never tasteth pangs:
> Treat it like a dead ground.[19]

The Sikh poetic tradition advises the individual faced with a situation of inevitable suffering, to accept it with a sense of resignation to the Divine Will. The only alternative is to engage oneself in prayer for the alleviation of suffering, not only from one's own life, but from the life of humanity at large:

> Save this burning world through
> Thy grace, O Lord!
> Lift us to whichever door of salvation
> Thou decidest.[20]

A Perspective on Death

"The death-theme affects the hedonist and voluptuary on the one hand and the devotee on the other in different ways according as either understands the fulfilment of life to consist in what he has been seeking." Thus observes Prof. Talib in the context of a study of Sheikh Farid's spiritual experience. To those who behold the underlying law of the universe in which all that is created is seen to be in a state of flux and subject to annihilation, "Death is a visible presence, not to be ignored in the course of the daily round of life." Says Farid:

> Life is like a tree growing on the river's
> bank - how long may it last?
> How long may the unbaked pitcher retain water?[21]

Compassion for man's state is the theme of another of Farid's couplets, wherein "Death is figured as the bridegroom who must carry away on the appointed day, his betrothed Bride, loth to leave the parents' home like the typical Indian Bride."[22] Guru Nanak employs the metaphor of sister and brother for depicting the relation of the body with the soul. At the time of parting, the 'sister' calls out to the 'brother', but the latter has become a stranger to her. She pines and burns in separation.[23]

The elements of inevitability and indeterminacy associated with Death, by no means exclusive to Sikh tradition, constitute two major themes of hymns dealing with evanescence of human life, in the *Guru Granth.* Guru Nanak refers to "death overtaking all, all being subject to separation."[24] Guru Arjan's expression – "whoever is born, is sure to die,"[25] lends support to modern existentialist contention that an infant at birth is old enough to die. Man, on this view, is a being-toward-death. Guru Tegh Bahadur, in his own pathos-filled style, affirms:

> Whoever comes into being, has to depart:
> If not today, may be tomorrow.[26]

The moment of the actual arrival of death is kept secret, though its inevitability is not. Sheikh Farid talks of the 'eagle' swooping unawares upon the crane, spoiling its fun and frolic. Guru Nanak speaks of the 'net' thrown in to catch the fish; that is how death appears all too suddenly. And one knows not the mode of one's departure, how painful or peaceful will the end be!

In his depiction of the existential man, Guru Nanak counts ten stages of life, beginning with the baby's love of mother's milk; followed by the various temptations and affections of life, leading to a decline in physical strength and finally to death that reduces the body to ashes.[27] The truism that no one is completely satiated with the measure of lifetime given to him or her, is expressed in one of his *Salokas*: "None seems to depart with the feeling that all his involvements are over." "Slowly and in bits, life is consumed and wasted away; death descends without asking and without giving a chance to complain."[28] Kabir strikes an optimistic note in proclaiming that it is through death alone that the eternal, perfect bliss is attained; that is why he is not afraid of death like the rest of mortals.[29] However, this assertion of Kabir need not be construed in isolation and in the literal sense. Death is welcome, as it comes, but death is no better than life according to the Sikh perspective in general. Human life is a serious affair; it is valuable gift, a rare opportunity to identify and realize the moral and spiritual objectives. That seems to be *Gurbani's* main thrust. It assures man that he is a the pinnacle of all creation; it reminds him that he is the embodiment of divine light itself.

An off-beat dimension of death and, for that matter, of life, is *Gurbani's* favourite conception of death-in-life. At the mundane level, it would sound queer and deserving of the cowards to say that one is as good as dead while alive; but in *Gurbani* this expression points to an awakened spirit fully aware of its origin and ultimate destiny. It refers to a person exercising control over his ego, over worldly attachments, over the sense of 'living' or 'being'. A hymn of Guru Amardas concludes with a paradox that puts the pith of the matter: The true life is attained by one who courts death-in-life, through recognition of the divine Ordinance, by divine Grace.[30] Kabir is in full agreement with this position, since he observes that whereas everyone dies sooner or later, no one really knows how to die. If we knew what it means to die we would not have to die again. The point is elaborated in Guru Nanak's hymn in *Ramakali* measure : We cannot realize the absolute truth as long as hope and fear bind us down. One who expects not amidst expectations, meets the Truth. That is the way to earn salvation; that is how to die while-alive.[31]

Nirmal Kumar Jain who applies to such a death the epithet of 'philosophic death' draws a parallel with *Nirvana* in its traditional sense. In Sikhism, it is 'dying out'. "But dying out of what?" he asks, and answers: "of *haumai*, the ego, the narrow self." For this, "one has to shake hands with death. It is not death of the body; it is death of the psyche, a much difficult thing."[32] Puran Singh in his poetic style describes Death as the bride of the brave. "Death, apparent death, is embraced by the Khalsa as no lover ever embraced his sweetheart. The Khalsa dies like the dashing waves of the sea, creating in the wake of its death millions more like itself." Citing Szirbi, the great Hungarian man of faith, Puran Singh approvingly remarks: "Death is the soul's realm, not of the body. Thou wilt see the soul there, just as thou seest it not here." "Death is a gate which all have to pass through. Beyond the gate is another courtyard, an unknown land." "He who is pure, his vision is clear, and he gazeth on death also with a smile."[33]

Viewed in the context of the ideal of service of humanity and the values which make the moral progress of society possible, suffering and death remain no more evils. The man of God tastes all sufferings as though these were *Amrita,* the ambrosial drink. He accepts sorrow and suffering, as they come, with perfect equanimity, with a sense of complete resignation to the Will divine. Inviting reference to Guru Nanak's hymn symbolically addressed to the black buck, Prof. Talib echoes the Guru's words : "Delicious are the delusions of the world."[34]

> Listen thou black buck,
> why art thou so absorbed in this orchard?
> The fruit of poison tastes sweet
> for a few days only;
> Then will it begin to torment thee...
> Pleasure is unstable like the stormy ocean;
> Like the flashing lightning...
> Believe Nanak thou black buck:
> forget not that thy path is the path of death![35]

Conquest of Suffering

In the Sikh poetic tradition, the concept of *Vijog* or alienation is associated with *dukh* or suffering, and the concept of *Sanjog* or union with *sukh,* i.e. joy and peace. Illustrations to this effect are rampant all over the corpus of the *Guru Granth.* Suffering or anguish may have multiple causes, but the assumption of individuated soul separated from its Base, pinpoints spiritual alienation as the root-cause of human suffering. Even though Sikhism does not proceed with the diagnosis and cure of the malady of suffering in the fashion of Buddhism, which lends medical flavour to the latter, the Sikh tradition does prescribe the method or *marga* of *Nam-simran* as comprehensive remedy for all the ills.

The dimension of *Sanjog-Vijog* pair of concepts that also forms the basis of Sikh mysticism, is the dimension of love-relation, which at the profane level is love between the spouses and at the sacred level, love of man for God. *Sanjog,* in the sense of de-alienation of the soul, is the culmination of this mysticism, which properly speaking is an experience and not a creed. As pointed out by Niharranjan Ray, there are many points of similarity and divergence between Guru Nanak and the totality of Indian medieval mystical tradition that is protestant and non-conformist. Guru Nanak's mysticism "was limited to the final goal of *sahaja* experience which at the ultimate analysis was a mystical, ineffable, unanalyzable, inexpressible experience." Basic in this discipline is the conquest of the mind and the final point in the ascent is the "state of mystic experience which is the Ultimate Reality itself."[36]

However, Sikhism shares with Indian mystics, in general, its concern for communication and union with the supreme Being. Reality of the mystic experience is affirmed on the basis of the testimony provided by its religious leaders and revered men of piety. However, it would not be correct to assert that mysticism is of central importance in Sikhism. In the context of Kabir's compositions, Karine Schomer observes: "Utterances pointing to the ecstasies of mystical experience are not totally absent" in Kabir's hymns incorporated in the *Guru Granth*, but they are "strikingly few in comparison with those found in the *Kabir Granthavali*." The Sikhs are appropriately described by her in terms of a "solid, moral, God-fearing religious community of householders" rather than mystics. Theirs is a "common-sense religion of inner sincerity and outer morality."[37] The intuitive vision of the Sikh does not make him 'solitary' in the sense of idiosyncratic.

Nor can Sikh mysticism be described in terms of rapture, transport or emotional outburst. At best, it is complete absorption of the individual in contemplation or *simran*, which, in the words of Puran Singh, is "the true Builder, the slow silent architect of the Soul." "*Simran* is the Law of Love. It is the holy manifestation of God in the martrix of matter."[38] The Sikh looks inward to draw inspiration from his spiritual resources, to experience joy and ecstasy in the midst of his worldly and domestic chores. Bhai Vir Singh dwells on the idea and experience of joyfulness. The root-metaphor of his poetry is *khera* (joy), just as the root-metaphor of Farid *Bani* is *dukh*. Perhaps the two are the obverse and converse sides of the same coin. Baba Farid flourished four centruries before the advent of Sikhism, and Bhai Vir Singh four centuries after it. This journey of eight hundred years is the journey from the idiom of suffering to the idiom of joy, in the interpretation of Sikh spirituality.

The joyful state in Bhai Vir Singh is no different from the blissful spiritual state of communion, which in his poetic diction is termed 'wasl' or '*milap*' – that is '*sanjog*' in its mystical dimension. His composition *Rana Surat Singh* concludes with the symbolic union of Rani Raj Kaur, deeply absorbed in loving devotion and attaining to the state of equipoise and merger (*sahaj-jog/sanjog*) equivalent to the status of Gurmukh, the God-oriented one.[39] That is the state of freedom from suffering and anguish, freedom from fear and anxiety, freedom from duality and *vijog*.

Guru Nanak indicates this state of realization and the means to its attainment, in unmistakable terms:

One who abandons the sinning self
and recognizes the Self
Afflict him neither sorrow
nor alienation, nor anguish.[40]

The self to abandon is ego, i.e. the sense of particularity; the Self to realize is Spirit, i.e. the immanent universality. For, "there is no cure for human suffering outside of man, as suffering is an inner ailment of the spirit," says Puran Singh. "All joy is the health of the Spirit... The inward strength comes from the regions of inspiration."[41]

Mysticism of spiritual union employs not only the symbol of sorrow-free, aguish-free state of the individual, but also the symbolism of a state that transcends all experience of pain and pleasure, sorrow and peace. This is clearly brought out in Guru Tegh Bahadur's hymns that depict the state of equipoise - where joy and suffering are treated alike, where affection and disaffection, honour and dishonour affect not one's equanimity. Such are the marks of a balanced being.[42] One of Guru Arjan's couplets addressed to Sheikh Farid speaks in the same vein:

O Faid, treat *dukh* and *sukh* alike
and cleanse the mind of evils,
Resigning thyself to Will divine,
arrive at His portal.[43]

An esoteric element in the *sanjoy-vijog* mysticism is the element of divine concern for the human destiny, known as grace or blessing. The Sikh poetic tradition makes eloquent references to the principle of divine grace operating in the human universe. Mystery of the divine Ordinance coupled with the mystery of Grace, belong to a realm that none can claim to penetrate. Here, reason only rationalizes, and faith alone serves and guides. In terms of the faith that *Gurbani* inculcates, grace of God descends on the elect, picked up by the hidden hand for final communion. The bride may lack winsome qualities, she may not possess merits prized by others, but if she is the recipient of her spouse's love and care, she is the fortunate one. It is she who attains *sanjog* with her Lord; she is *suhagan* and she is *suchaji*. All the others who fail to receive the glance of grace of the spouse, are the luckless ones, waiting for their turn; they suffer in *vijog* and the epithets of *duhagan* and *kuchaji* apply to them.

Says Nanak, when the glance gracious
blesses one,
All the miseries of *vijog* vanish.[44]

NOTES

1. *Adi-Granth* (Var Majh), p.149.
2. Karine Schomer in *Sikh Studies* (ed.Juergensmeyer and Barrier), Berkeley, 1979, p.84.
3. *Adi-Granth*, p.1102.
4. *Ibid*, p.517.
5. *Ibid.* p.1256.
6. See Arbaugh, *Kierkegaard's Authorship,* Allen and Unwin, 1968, 0.175.
7. G.S.Talib, *Guru Nanak : His Personality and Vision*, 1969, p.230.
8. L.M.Joshi, Journal of Religious Studies, Spring 1978, Patiala, p.72.
9. S.K.Chattopadhyaya, *Quest for Truth* (ed. K.K.Mittal), Delhi, 1976, p.498.
10. *Adi-Granth*, p.226.
11. *Ibid.* (Sloka Farid 81), p.1382.
12. Cf. Wazir Singh, *Philosophy of Sikh Religion*, Delhi, 1981, p.118.
13. *Adi-Granth*, (Sloka Farid : 41), p.1380.
14. *Kierkegaard's Authorship, op.cit.*, p.176.
15. G.S.Talib, *op.cit.*,p.232.
16. *Ibid.*, p.229.
17. *Adi-Granth*, p.5.
18. Karl Jaspers, *Philosophy,* Vol.2, Chicago, 1970(1932), p.203.
19. Adi-Granth, p.1379.
20. *Ibid*, p.853.
21. *Ibid*, p.1382
22. Gurbachan Singh Talib, *Perspectives on Sheikh Farid* (ed. G.S.Talib), Patiala, 1975, pp.93-4.
23. *Adi-Granth*, p.935.
24. *Ibid.*, p.595.
25. *Ibid.*, p.375.
26. *Ibid., p.1428.*
27. *Ibid.*, p.137.
28. *Ibid.*, p.1412.
29. *Ibid., p.1365.*
30. *Ibid.*, p.555.
31. *Ibid.*, p.877.
32. N.K.Jain, *Sikh Religion and Philosophy,* New Delhi, 1979, p.109.
33. Puran Singh, *Spirit of the Sikh*, Patiala, 1978, pp.89;58-0.
34. G.S.Talib, op.cit., pp.232-44.
35. Adi-Granth, p.439.
36. Niharranjan Ray, *The Sikh Gurus and the Sikh Society, 1975, pp.39,97.*
37. Karine Schomer, *op.cit.*, pp.84-6.
38. Puran Singh, *op.cit.*, p.28.
39. *Bhai Vir Singh Rachnavali,* vol.I, Patiala, 1972, p.389.

40. Adi-Granth, p.935.
41. Puran Singh, *op.cit.*, p.36.
42. Cf. Wazir Singh, *Falsafa te Sikh Falsafa*, Patiala, 1980, p.99.
43. *Adi-Granth*, p.1383.
44. *Ibid.*, p.955.

A PERSPECTIVE ON DONATION (DASWANDH)

A custom among the Sikhs, requiring one-tenth portion of one's earning to be donated for the community's welfare, is known as *daswandh.* Broadly speaking, it is a form of charity adopted since the time of Guru Ram Das who enjoined upon every follower of the faith to set apart a minimum of ten percent of the household's annual income for social uplift and for the on-going projects of the community. The fourth Guru was then engaged in having the holy tanks at Amritsar dug up, to be followed by the construction of Harimandir, the Golden Temple, and establishment of the township that developed into the city of Amritsar. The custom was strengthened by Guru Arjan who succeeded his father, Guru Ram Das, and saw to the completion of the projects involving huge amounts of money and other means.

Daswandh as part of the Sikh way of life, was originally conceived in its initial form, by the third Guru, Amar Das, to whose mature vision goes the credit of institutionalizing various customs and bringing about reforms, leading to the establishment of a distinct identity of the Sikhs as a social entity. It was Guru Amar Das who for the first time set up Sikh dioceses, known as *manjis*, 22 in number. He also established the institution of *masands* (viceregents) in order to collect contributions from the Sikhs associated with the *manjis*. These contributions were voluntary in spirit, even though made under the inspiration of the Guru, and subsequently becoming an article of the Sikh faith in the form of *daswandh.* The institution of Masand was finally wound up, in 1698, by Guru Gobind Singh who found that corrupt practices had crept into the system.

The tradition of *daswandh* has been kept alive, during the four centuries of its history, by the devout Sikhs, who faithfully donate one-tenth of their gross earnings (or even more) to a *guru-dwara* of their choice. The fund collected is utilized in the administration of services rendered to the community, in the form of free kitchen, dwelling units for pilgrims, educational institutions and of course helping the destitute. Daswandh augments the resources of the *guru-dwara* managements, otherwise built up on the basis of voluntary offerings made by visitors, both in cash and kind (in most cases, cash). As happens in such cases, deviation from the custom is widespread, mainly on account of the obligation to pay taxes, including income-tax, to the State exchequer. Even though no substitute for the religiously enjoined *daswandh*, donations and charities for the welfare of national and international community, made by the conscientious citizen, bring satisfaction to the donor of having done his/her duty by society.

Clearly, *daswandh* and the tax are distinct obligations of the Sikh as member of the religious community and as citizen of the State. One cannot replace the other. Similar distinction was apparent in the case of *zakat* and *jezia*, traditionally applied by the Muslims. Whereas the former (*zakat*) has been the religious commitment on the part of a Muslim, governed by the Quranic injunction to set apart one-fortieth of income for welfare activities, the other, viz. *jezia*, was a special tax imposed upon the non-believers for claiming protection from the Muslim rulers. The Arabic *zakat* originally meant 'purification' and came to mean purification of one's wealth by disbursing $2\frac{1}{2}\%$ of it every year for the destitute and poor. The percentage of *zakat* varied from case to case, being one animal (sheep or goat) for the owner of five camels, 5 % of the value of horses for the owner of a fleet (other than war-horses) and different rates for other types of wealth including gold, silver and household articles. In modern times several modifications have been proposed, as for instance the *zakat* to be paid into a "revolving fund" which would be expended in "income-producing enterprises," ultimately for the benefit of certain categories of the needy.

As for the *jezia*, it was a tax (rather octroi) to be paid by non-Muslim pilgrims in exchange for the protection received from the State administration. The rationale behind *jezia* was that whosoever did not accept Islam, was liable to be killed, but might be spared if he paid the prescribed tax (women and children being exempted). Aurangzeb, the sixth Muhgal Emperor of India, ordered that non-Muslims should pay this tax personally in the Court. A *kafir*, i.e. non-believer, was not permitted to wear a dress like the Muslim. The Sikh society had no paralled custom, though the principle of *daswandh* bore partial similarity with the Muslim *zakat* and *sadaqa*.

Daswandh as the ten-percent share of one's income to be given in charity, broadly resembles the Biblical injunction of Tithe which literally meant 'tenth part' of the farm produce, made applicable by the Church of England, for the support of parish priests. The Sikh farmers are known to have carried a part of their foodgrains, most often wheat, to the *langar* of a *guru-dwara*, by way of *daswandh* in kind. The gesture falls in line with the Semitic faiths prescribing a proportion of one's wealth to be offered as *zakat* or *tithe*. Classical Indian society had no set procedure for regulating donations or charities, even if oblique references are found, notably in Prashar Rishi's writings, urging the householder to offer 1/21 (for a brahmin, 1/31) part of income for the sake of 'gods'. Bhagavadgita and Upanishads commend 'true alms' given with a sense of duty in a fit place and time to a deserving person from whom one expects nothing in return.

The Sikh custom of *daswandh* was codified in the Rehatnamas written during the lifetime of Guru Gobind Singh, or soon after. For instance, Bhai Nand Lal issues the directive: "Earn your livelihood and put a tenth part of it in the mouths of Sikhs." The Sikh tradition, with its stress on Nam, Dan, Ishnan (contemplation, charity, cleanliness), as also on *kirat* (earning one's livelihood through honest means) and 'sharing', has always held the virtues of compassion, service and benevolence as integral to its ethical code. However, almsgiving or begging has never been promoted or regulated by custom. Charity as a principle of sharing is upheld by the Sikhs, even as the Christians take to the theology of charity as the 'form' of all virtues, manifesting itself in the organizations such as Sisters of Charity, the Red Cross, and in noble souls like Mother Teresa. *Daswandh* is but a concrete expression of the spirit of charity and benevolence.

THE SIKH VIEW OF PUNJAB'S CULTURE

Punjabi culture is the style of life based upon the tradition of Punjab's thought-art-morals complex. Its humanistic orientation is located in values considered supreme for the advancement of both the individual and community. The elements of culture which in their totality constitute 'Punjabiyat' (Punjabiness), are the elements that differentiate Punjabi culture from other cultures, and determine its uniqueness. The geographical situation of the Punjab has been and continues to be such as to keep the people's life open to influences of the Eastern and Western civilizations, life-styles and ideologies. Nevertheless, Punjab has maintained the basic ingredients of its people's intellectual, emotional and social focus within the framework of Punjabiyat, which can readily be identified in the multi-dimensional community of aspirations, rites and ceremonies, literature and arts, social and moral relations, religious and philosophical beliefs as well as values and ideals of the Punjabi people settled in every corner of the world.

Culture with its intimate relation with people's life, cannot be conceived independently of human elements and traits. Man's affection and care for other human beings, spirit of sharing and working for the reduction of human suffering and anguish, desire to help fellow-beings in a spirit of service, are among the motives and endeavours replete with humanitarian intent. But, the sense in which 'humanism' has evolved as an ideology, faith and philosophy, is distinct from this spirit of service and love (i.e. humanitarianism). Humanism as a movement and thought in its own right, has firm faith in the human capability for the comprehensive development of mankind, in its individual and collective forms. However, Punjabi culture attempts a synthesis of humanism with faith in God. For, theism is the pivot around which the Punjabi thought in its entirety has revolved. The land of Five Rivers has been the home of ancient and medieval religious faiths, commentaries of sacral texts, Vedic compositions and epics, Bhakti (devotional) lore and hagiography, *Gurbani* and its schools of interpretation. Not only do its literary genres, romantic verse and drama, traditional prose and modern experiments bear the stamp of religion, but also its various art-forms–painting, sculpture, architecture, music and dance are so embossed.

In the interpretation of Punjab's culture, the concept and figure of 'five' has a key-role to play. The 'Punjab' derives its nomenclature from 'panj' (5) and 'aab' (water/rivers). The spirit of Punjabiyat, too, is the product of its five dimensional categories, viz., the physico-economic, intellectual, aesthetic, moral and spiritual aspects.

(1) The Physical dimension of Punjabi Culture

Ever since the advent of Guru Nanak, the history of Punjab has been intertwined with the Sikh-history. In the contemporary world, a Sikh is the acknowledged representative of Punjabi people and a symbol of Punjabiyat. The importance of physical culture in the Punjabi way of life is at once noticed on having a glimpse of the well-built, agile and impressive bearing of a handsome *Sardar ji* with rural background, particularly when he is attired in a well-tailored outfit or uniform, complete with a nicely tied turban. Arenas, physical exercises, strenuous games (like *kabaddi*) and swings (*peengh*) have made significant contribution in the Punjab's life tradition, resulting in the infatuation of Punjabi young men and women for physical fitness and health. On the basis of this very physical stamina have the battles been fought and won; and to this physical culture did Professor Puran Singh offer a tribute, when the said :

> Hail to the lion-hearted youth!
> No work, no task to perform:
> Miles of brisk walk –
> just to exercise the legs.

In the good old days, the Punjab was known for its leafy dish and butter-milk (*saag-lassi*), corn loaves and bread. In the name of such blessings used the citizens of Punjab to say: 'life' is led in the Punjab, all else is false. The city-civilization, in particular the Western-type technological advances, have on one had offered the Punjabi people modern amenities and privileges, but have on the other hand, robbed their traditional life-style of several of the invaluable blessings. Whereas in the former days, quantity of milk in the average Punjabi's diet was the highest in the country, nowadays the per capita consumption of liquor has risen to the top. However, implicit faith in the make-up of Punjabi character is surely indicative of the fact that the Punjabi is alive to his destiny, and would not permit himself to be pushed to the wall.

The Punjabi is fond of affluence in his material life. He has excelled all targets in the farm-production and ushered in an era of prosperity. If he did not find the circumstances favourable for turning a big industrialist, he could not be left behind in the field of small-scale industry and handicrafts. Where is the machine which he has not fabricated on his lathe, and which is the spare part of Japanese or German make whose replica is beyond his daring and common sense? To accept every challenge, to resist all undue pressure, is intrinsic to the Punjabi character.

No doubt, motives of spreading the spiritual message and quest for Truth formed the background of Guru Nanak's missionary journeys, but touring through the motherland and abroad was an unmistakable indication of the Punjabi's extrovert inclinations. Newer pastures and newer economic ventures have always had a pull for the Punjabi – taking him to all corners of the world, be it Canada or New Zealand, Siberia or Sudan. Sociability and capacity for adapting themselves to conditions, have equipped the inhabitants of the Punjab to settle in foreign climes with fortitude and success. The Punjabi community, on the basis of rich experience gained in the past, has evolved certain 'formulas' – such as "one who defies, falls" (indicative of the Punjabi's tendency to overwhelm and dominate others) and "try to make the opponent submit, if he doesn't, do so yourself" – speak of his down-to-earth, pragmatic approach. And it is also true that, if the son of Punjabi soil has earned the admiration of white and black nationalities alike, at places he has created a considerable mess as well.

A robust sense of the day-to-day material life, of its economic mechanism, of its family-cum-social ties, of its international relations, of its professions of faith and morals, – awareness of all these facets of life, – is the first major step in the direction of Punjabi humanism. Nature is the home of man; to be able to feel at home in any nook and corner of it, to feel its heart-throb, is the primary value of Punjabi culture. The supremacy of man in this world of "eighty-four lakhs" of species, has been alluded to in this quotation from Gurbani: "All other creatures only slave for you/You are the overlord of this earth" - (Guru Granth, p.372). If the cosmic principles operate in the physical world, the law of "each action considered on its merit" operates in the human world. This is the realm of righteousness, - a humanistic gift of Guru Nanak to the Punjabi culture.

(2) The Intellectual aspect of Punjabiyat

If we look at it from a comparative perspective, the tradition of Punjab's inhabitant has not been of an intellectual, but of a "rustic" - even if he holds a degree in laws, or serves as a college lecturer after acquiring the master's degree. Yet, even the rustic utterings and deeds of the Punjabi are full of disguised implications, because he is endowed with common sense in good measure. The Punjabi admits that he does not part with a sugar-cane, but may offer a solid piece of jaggery; but it does not prove that he fails to watch his interest; instead, it indicates the generosity that colours his unsophisticated thinking. He does not believe in cunning or craftiness, the more he tries to be smart or clever, the more does he drift away from his "Punjabiness". He asks - "Why involve oneself in complications? Why not to lead a straight-forward, simple life?"

And yet, "intelligence is a great gift indeed;" "without wit life is empty." The Gurus have exclaimed - "Through intelligence comtemplate the Lord, through intelligence win a place of honour." How can a Punjabi be devoid of practical wisdom when he has imbibed the teachings of "keeping passions in check, and reason supreme," and "the lesson of all education – not to entangle oneself with a fool," from the very beginning? It the saints and bhaktas raised the banner of devotion to God, in the Punjab, the Gurus laid stress on rationality along side loving devotion. The Punjabi is thoughtful when it is time to think, he is contemplative in the hour of devotion, and a simple, unpretentious being at other times.

Punjabi culture has been witness to utmost refined and profound thinking. The intellectual giants of this land produced the ancient treasures of wisdom, composed Vedic hymns, and created texts like the Mahabharta. The enlightened pandits of this soil have charmed the hearts and minds of the people, the bhatts have written historical accounts in their own way, the great Panini laid down the principles of grammar, mathematicians and scientists have earned acclaim in the field of intellect. The scared writings of Guru Granth and Dasam Granth are the unique gifts of Punjab.

The Punjabi psyche has indeed been blessed with expansiveness and versatility of the cosmic creation. The variegated and multi-dimensional worldly creation has been depicted in the profound expressions like - "millions are the under-worlds/millions float in space," and "numerous be the Indras, moons, numerous suns and stars/many the lands and countries many, many the regions afar" - (*Japuji*). The Dasam-Granth compositions are not only an instance of the poetic excellence, depicting a panorama of nations and nationalities, continents and regions, languages, dialects, weapons, literary marvels, sects, professions, arts and so on, but also a formidable treasure of knowledge relating to endless cosmic existence and colourful variety of human life. If the extent of the wide expanding universe, whose concept takes shape in the human mind through such writings, exerts to make the mental universe of man equally wide and expansive, all acerbities and acrimonies of human life would disappear. It is in such a spirit that humanistic thinkers have conceived the oneness of a single, universal human race, the *homo-sapiens*.

The colourful variety and multiplicity of cosmic existence is one side of the picture, its wholeness and unicity present the other side. When the human intellect forms the concept of unity in diversity, when the meanings of "It is many, and yet It is one" dawn in the mind, the rational faculty is set on its course to the ultimate heights. Punjabi culture, in the context of the entire Indian thought, has conceived the ideal of supreme knowledge in the concept of Brahman (the Absolute). The human consciousness, when it is in the tune with the Brahman, shapes the resident of the Realm of Knowledge, in the form of Brahman-gyani, i.e. one in possession of absolute knowledge. Replete with the richness of his mystic experience, this 'divine' human being is the one with "benevolence springing eternal in his mind," and is the Messiah of mankind.

(3) The Aesthetic Aspect

In the Punjabi culture, intellect and aesthetic enjoyment go side by side. If the ideal of rational activity is absolute or cosmic knowledge, the goal of aestheticism is blissfulness and ecstasy. The sense of beauty in the individual's life initiates with handsome physique, impressive outfit and charming outlook; upkeep and cleanliness of the environs speak of his aesthetic taste. Dynamism of the Punjabi is the creative dimension, which has been termed as the Realm of Creativity, in the Japuji. Promotion of higher values in life is the humanistic aspect of this very activism.

Another feature of the creative impulse of Punjabi people is the adornment and decoration displayed at the fairs and festivals of the Punjab. Be it the Baisakhi of Amritsar, or be it the Basant (Spring festival) of Patiala or Chheharta, the words of Dhaniram Chatrik truly depict the spirit:

> With flute under his armpit,
> it is joy all around –
> The Punjabi joins the fair
> making hilarious sounds.

Fond of the fair, the village damsel with tinklets around her ankles, appears into the town, and lo! the city-stars fade in front of her lunar glow. A Punjabi festival stands for enjoyment, for the carefree spirit of youth, for life full of colour, for longings, for taste, – and the dust and dirt of the fair-site is engulfed by the brightness of bangles, by the rhythm of folk couplets. The Punjabi culture can scarcely be conceived without reference to the young girls' gatherings and dances, religious festivals and processions, night-long singing sessions, celebrations and get-togethers.

Punjab's artistic beauty emerges from the soil of Punjab. The materials that go into the making of earthen pots and toys, the thread used in the embroidery and flowery apparel, the flora for garlands, the wood used in the production of colourful beds and furniture – all are gifts of the ground. The love-story of the Punjab is the tale of Sohni's water-pitcher, the story of Kaido's stolen *choori.* All its arts and crafts, poetry and paintings, tell the tales of Punjab's soil. Professor Puran Singh designates Sohni's statue as the symbol of Punjabiyat.

Those who view the Punjabi culture through its 'cultural' eves and nights, are not far wrong. When the *bhangra* dance-form goes on with the drum-beat, when the *giddha* of girls proceeds with the tempo of tunes, when musical measures support the songs, when instruments are played upon and folk-forms of drama staged, - it is the people's life that makes the presentation. The audiences become alive to all the longings and desires, the anxieties and fears, the dreams and ideals of the young boys and girls. The Punjab has gifted to its poetic measures the songs of both sorrow and pleasure, to its music the compositions of Gurbani and musical styles, to its ballads the Heers, Sassis and Mirzas. Here, there is no dearth of heroic songs, nor of composers; neither of 'wondrous dramas', nor of spiritual verses.

The conjunction of intellect and aesthetic sense produces a state of the mind wherein the individual turns knower and enjoyer all at once. He is the thinker, he the devotee; envisions he the Divine, enjoys he His presence. Out of the material of reason and sensibility are restructured the individual's sense and mind, intellect and intuition, making him an inhabitant of the angelic realms. Day and night, he remains absorbed in contemplation. Here it is the bliss, here the mood of ecstasy and rapture.

(4) The Ethical Aspect

The ethical aspect of Punjab's culture is in fact the moral-social aspect, for ethics operates in a social framework. An individual totally divorced from the human community, stranded on a desolate island like a Robinson Crusoe, may be eking out his existence, with his actions not subject to any moral judgement as right or wrong etc. But normally, the first manifestation of morality as one's behaviour and conduct in relation to his associates, is indicative of his social attitude. The Punjabi custom of social interchange and courtesy is embedded in its own tradition, even if its open-mined character appears informal in contrast with Lucknow style decencies. At any rate, the 'welcome' greeting of the Punjabi has its own peculiar warmth and sincerity.

Another characteristic of the Punjabi morality is the spirit of cooperation and helpfulness. The existing situation of any community is the outcome of the wisdom and follies on the part of its forebears. The impact on the Punjabi life and tradition of the seventeenth and eighteenth century struggles and sacrifices is still perceptible. This tradition was brought into being by the valiant spirit of those men of action who, in the terminology of Guru Nanak, are described as the courageous-adventurous-crusaders. A Punjabi who does not protest against wanton violence and injustice, and fails in his duty to protect the underdog, certainly lacks in the degrees of Punjabiyat.

Even as the value of individual life is essential to moral advancement, no ethical progress can be anticipated by divorcing it from the truly humanistic spirit. The socially oriented qualities and virtues occupy a place of honour in a healthy moral outlook. In the evolution of Punjab's culture, the commandments of honest labour and sharing of one's earnings have made a rich contribution. The development of virtues like contentment and temperance, benevolence and kindliness, courage and justfulness are potent enough to lend humanistic orientation to the Punjabi personality. The Gurus (spiritual mentors) have inculcated the lesson of non-attachment all right, but of renunciation not in the least.

The pinnacle of Punjabi humanism comprises the ideal which in the Sikh form of prayer is called the 'well-being of all'. The ideal finds its spontaneous expression in the quotation-"None is my enemy, none alien to me; in peace can I live with all." And when Guru Amar Das prayed –

> Save this burning world, O Lord,
> Through Thy Act of Grace!
> Save the people through the path
> They may choose to take –

he prayed for the entire humanity, and not for one particular class or community. Humanism takes in its embrace the whole of mankind, without a cleavage or distinction. This healthy and living tradition has strength enough to put the deflecting or deviating Punjabis back on the righteous path.

The spiritual basis of Punjabi morality consists in contemplation, and its active expression in service. The individual activated by inner inspiration through contemplation, dedicates himself to his duty, – at times as a valiant soul, at time as a devotee, at times as a generous benefactor. The son of Punjab's soil, blessed with the gifts of contemplation and service, and conscious of his heritage, takes to the set of values that include common sense and spiritual awareness, bliss and ecstasy, as also emancipation-in-life. The ideal man of Punjabi morality is not the 'realized soul' or *siddha* retiring to the hills. He is but the man of active life, in communication with his companions, sharing with them his sense of values; he emancipates himself and helps others to that end.

(5) The Spiritual Aspect

Covering the physical, intellectual, artistic and moral stages, the Punjabi culture proceeds to its spiritual objectives. In conformity with the Punjabi character, first stage in the spiritual journey is the adoption of an attitude of meeting the plaints of God, as it were. From this angle, bhakti (devotion) is just one of the tasks to be performed sooner or later in the day. Getting up in the morning, attend to the business of prayer, beseeching the Divine to supervise all the errands the day long. As for oneself, there won't be any time to remember Him, being busy with operating the tractor, or dealing with the customer, or teaching the pupils!

The next stage in the religious life is made up of faith in the efficacy of prayer. The Punjabi banks on the belief-"whatever I seek of my Lord, that is bestowed upon me." Meditation becomes a part of his life-style. With every breath, he says his prayers: for the casting away of his fears and anxieties, for the seeking of blessings. As his communion with the Godhead becomes deeper, his self-reliance keeps on growing.

At the further stage of spiritual life, the seeking of the Punjabi turns into inquisitiveness about the problem of faith. What is the meaning of religious teaching, what the scripture has to say? The tradition of gnostic circles has had a long past in the Punjabi folk-life. The interpretive schools of Bani (scriptural compositions) are as significant a part of Punjabi culture as the scholastic works on the ancient aphorisms or schools of philosophy in the context of India as a whole. Being the philosophy of Religion, this rational dimension of faith bears the stamp of scholars' approval, from the pedagogic perspective.

But, ratiocination or philosophy is not the be-all and end-all. Beyond the realm of reason, religion is a matter for the inner depths, where friendly links are fostered within the region of emotion, when tranquillity is attained, when automatic contemplation goes on. In such a state of the mind, sometimes, even the rules and regulations of piety are thrown overboard:

> Not to talk of disciplines any more!
> Running away from the do'es and don'ts,
> No regard for principles and rules –
> drowning all thought! (Puran Singh)

The Punjabi not only ploughs the field, not only operates the loom, not only acts as commission-agent, but indulges in mystic raptures in turn. He has his tryst with the Infinite, the joyful experience of identification with the Timeless.

The Punjabi culture has bestowed upon the ideal person the title of *gurmukh* (the God-oriented man of piety), the highest reach of humanism. The 'gurmukh' maintains steady relation between the worldly and the spiritual; he crosses over from one realm into the other fearlessly. He has awareness of the truth, knowledge of love and consciousness of the Divine Ordinance. He hears the rivers of Punjab sing the sublime Japuji of Nanak. Humanity throbs with his heart-beats, and in his vision is present the motto: "Recognize all Mankind as One."

THE VISION OF A SIKH THEOLOGIAN

Bhai Jodh Singh is a theologian of the Sikh faith. This conclusion emerges from the tasks undertaken and performed by him during a century of lifetime (1882-1981). Whatever else he did in the various spheres of life - personal, professional, public - does not bear the impress of his personality as much as his contribution to the interpretation and advocacy of the spiritual texts and tenets of Sikhism. He adopts the posture of authority when it comes to exposition of a passage from the Guru Granth, his opinions taking an air of finality and claiming to be as near to the original as possible. The Sikh intelligentsia of the contemporary period not only has acquiesced in the stance so adopted but has bestowed upon him the honorific title of *Bhai Sahib,* shared by another luminary in the field, Bhai Vir Singh.

To the areas of Sikh theology and exegesis, Bhai Jodh Singh brought the quality of precision, a necessary characteristic of mathematics that was his basic discipline. His expositions of Gurbani texts are marked by fewness of words; his explanations are shorn of verbiage and conform to a pattern that has maintained a surprising uniformity over three quarters of a century. The idiom he employed in, say, 1909, is remarkably similar to the idiom of his subsequent writings up to the late seventies. In his exegetical works, he has maintained a style of his own, that of paraphrasing the poetic text, using a minimum of words, almost repeating the original passage in prose. Instances of this are abundantly available in his widely circulated *GurmatNirnay,* in Punjabi, and several of his expository works of *tika-kari.* It is only when he attempt to philosophize an issue that he indulges in the luxury of creative interpretation and quotes passages from carefully selected works bearing upon the topic under discussion. Of course, all his quotations and citations have one orientation, namely, intelligent defence of his religions beliefs.

In the role of a theologian, Bhai Jodh Singh endeavors to present Sikhism in the most favourable light possible, without indulging in polemics. Even when he is writing under the title of 'philosophy of Sikhism', at bottom he remains a theologian committed to the canons of his faith. His religious philosophy is a variation of his defence of the beliefs and injunctions of Sikhism, supported by a measure of ratiocination. He does not pretend to assume the posture of neutrality or objectivity in order to impress his readers of a 'philosophic' bearing. To use an expression of Paul Tillich,[1] all his philosophy is concealed theology.

The Young Interpreter

In a recent reprint[2] of 'Babu Jodh Singh's' speech given in the Convention of Religions held in 1909, Bhai Sahib seeks to sum up the Sikh creed in four words: unity, equality, faith and love. He bases the idea of unity on the concept of singleness of the Divine symbolized by the numeral '1' at the beginning of the Mul Mantra. The formless shining through all the forms is the belief inspired by the Guru's word. God as the existing reality is not to be understood as an abstract idea, but is a matter of experience as opposed to intellect. The problem for man is to find the way to salvation. The 'path of discipleship' that Sikhism literally is, indicates the solution in as much as the necessity of a guru is emphasized. Guru, in Sikhism, is not an incarnation of the Deity, but a 'servant' of the Lord taking birth in order to infuse spiritual life in human beings. After the ascension of ten Gurus, the Sikhs recognize the Granth as the repository of their teachings, equivalent to the guru. The young interpreter of the Sikh faith categorically states: "In reality we do not believe in any salvation attainable after death. We must be saved in this life."[3]

In the speech just cited, Bhai Jodh Singh toys with the concepts of existence and individuality, not only in relation to God, but in relation to man. He concludes that with the destruction of individuality, existence does not cease. In the case of God, creation is the manifestation of his individuality, and with cessation of creation, individuality is destroyed, though existence remains intact. Similarly, with the destruction of individuality in man, existence does not cease. This is an interesting philosophical puzzle, but Bhai Sahib refrains from elaborating it or making his views explicit any further.

On the issue of transmigration of the soul, Bhai Sahib makes the assertion that "we believe in it," as also in the law of Karma, though "our karma is annihilated when we take shelter with the Guru."[4] The skeptical scholar who is inclined to contest these doctrines, can scarcely afford to view the assertion of Bhai Jodh Singh lightly or any the less seriously.

Sikh Philosophy

The distinctly marked second stage of the theological career of Bhai Sahib is noticed in his contribution captioned 'Sikh Philosophy' to the volume[5] sponsored by Government of India and first published in 1952. The concise metaphysical statement made in the essay reads: "God is; He has created by His own power man and Universe, and the ultimate object of human life if to realize the Truth; this is, in substance, the Sikh doctrine."[6] The Sikh gurus were definitely opposed to polytheistic or henotheistic ideas, according to Bhai Sahib. They were outspoken exponents of monotheism. Reference to numeral 1 (one) and its implications re-occurs in this essay, coupled with Bhai Sahib's version of the Mul Mantra. The spiritual philosophy of the Gurus is to be found in the outpourings of the divinely inspired hearts, that is, in the hymns born of an inner illumination. Insistence on the need of a true guru for helping men out of despair and helplessness, is repeated with the support of quotations from the scripture. However the point is made that it is not the body of the guru that is the guru; it is his word that is the guru. Hence obeisance to the guru's body or the guru's *darshan* does not bring any merit to the disciple.

A departure in the essay of 1952 over the speech of 1909, consists in the references to the ideas of immanence and transcendence of God reconciled to each other, and to the *vijog-sanjog* pair which "runs the whole gamut of life." Sanjog is also interpreted as the union of the soul with God, effected through a life of active service in which *sat-sang, kirtan* and *nam*-meditation play an important part.

Bhai Jodh Singh explicates a passage from Guru Angad's hymn concerning *haumai*,[7] wherein the ego is described as a "deep-rooted malady," "but there is a remedy for its also." The actual wording of the hymn gives the impression as if the remedy of the chronic malady of egoism lay in the ego itself. And a number of interpreters have explained the passage on these lines. But Bhai Sahib disagrees and puts forth his alternative explanation.

The essay is remarkable for its meaningful brevity and lucidity, and succeeds in introducing the inquisitive reader to the basic tenets of the religious philosophy of Sikhism. It avoids the technical terminology of logic and metaphysics and uses a minimum of argument to build up its case. It relies mostly on the text from which passages are freely quoted to illustrate the point at issue. Rather, the points for discussion are dawn from the scriptural text itself, and the whole essay is in the spirit of rational defence and justification of the beliefs held on faith. Herein lies the role of Bhai Jodh Singh as a Silkh theologian.

Philosophy and Religion

As late as 1979, two university teachers of Canada edited and published a book in the field of comparative religion, to which Bhai Sahib contributed an article entitled 'Guru Nanak's Religion and Philosophy'.[8] The article is a rehash of the earlier works, except that it attempts to define philosophy and religion and then condense the Sikh thought into the framework laid out. For his definitions, Bhai Sahib leans heavily on the work edited by Dr Radhakrishnan, with an introduction by Maulana Abul Kalam Azad.[9] The purpose of philosophic quest, on this view, is to find out the meaning of life and existence, through systematic speculation. "The problem of religion arises from the realization of the imperfect condition of man," he says quoting Radhakrishnan.[10] The aim is to have an abiding union with God, through intuitive experience. Guru Nanak was not a 'philosopher' in the sense noted above, but he was essentially a religious man, according to Bhai Sahib.

The body of the article is replete with paraphrases of the scriptural passages, gleaned from the compositions of Guru Nanak, supported by verses of Bhai Gurdas. The monotheistic outlook of Guru Nanak is shown to be in line with the traditional Indian thought, rather than resulting from the Islamic influence. References are also made to the six Darshans in order to distinguish Guru Nanak's position from the respective systems in regard to the existence of God and his attributes, and the nature of human soul. In the Advaitic thought of Shankra, "Isvara is said to be associated with cosmic maya, while the individual is associated with *avidya* or ignorance."[11] Guru Nanak, however, asserts that all souls are created by God, and all are the same in essence. For all human beings, there is only one Dharam, and that is to practise truth, to do the righteous deeds. "A tree is known from the fruit it bears, so a man's religion is known from the deeds he performs," concludes Bhai Sahib.[12] The religion of Guru Nanak teaches man that the true purpose of life will be gained by submitting to the Will of the Ordainer.

Indian Religious Thought

In between the second and the third stages marked above, Bhai Jodh Singh was commissioned by the University at Patiala, in 1966, to give a set of four lectures in the series of Guru Nanak Commemorative Lectures.[13] Bhai Sahib posed the question: what contribution did Guru Nanak make to the Indian religious thought? And proceeded to answer it in his lectures, starting with a review of the ancient Indian thought. He makes a rapid survey of the Vedic mantras, Upanishadic insights, the Jaina and Buddhist faiths, and the Nyaya, Visheshika and Sankhya speculations, in chaste Punjabi. In the second lecture, he discusses the Yoga discipline of

Patanjali, Hath-Yoga of Gorakh Nath and traces the background of the Natha sect. Quoting extensively from the compositions of Gorakh Nath, he explains some of the intricacies of the yogic thought, praxis and terminology. This was a lively subject for the Punjabi audience. The similarities of phrases, expressions and stanzas between Gorakh-Bani and Guru-Bani are at once striking and interesting.

The third lecture in the series deals with Mimamsa and Vedantic schools. In the latter, Bhai Sahib discusses the Advaitic thought of Shankra, and the five other sub-schools of Vedanta. His summary of all this huge material is remarkable in itself; it does not omit any significant issue and yet confines itself to the limits of one lecture. The last of the four lectures delineates the religious though of Guru Nanak, of course, in the familiar tone and style of Bhai Sahib, fortified by comparative insights here and there. How far do these lectures succeed in propounding a new philosophical system, or in holding out a new vision of life? The answer is not so very encouraging, and so the quest continues. Bhai Sahib remains content with making categorical statements, based upon his reading of the Guru-Bani; for instance: "The foundation of a religious life is ethical conduct."[14] "Guru Nanak has accepted the doctrine of Karma and transmigration."[15] "This obstacle (the evil) in the way to spiritual progress has been put by Himself. ... The soul attains to the Supreme State through overcoming such impediments."[16]

The Leading Exponent

In the quincentenary year of Guru Nanak's birth, 1969, the Guru Nanak Foundation published a booklet by Dr Bhai Jodh Singh, which consists of extracts from his earlier writings compiled and edited for the occasion.[17] Similar short works based upon the lectures and discourses given by him at different universities and institutions have also appeared, but they do not contain any new material. These publication, however, testify to his position as the leading exponent of Sikhism of the contemporary period. Of course, the most outstanding and major work that contributed to this reputation of Bhai Sahib was his *Gurmat Nirnay,* published in the early thirties.[18]

Bhai Jodh Singh takes up fourteen issues for discussion in *Gurmat Nirnay,* most of them of theoretical and ideological interest. The topics include Akal Purakh (the Non-temporal Being); the phenomenal creation; man; the purpose of individual life; the True Guru; the unstruck melody; and the Khalsa. They also included the rather controversial subjects of

Transmigration, Karma and Miracles. The book breaks new ground in the field of Sikh religious philosophy. Apart from being an impressive specimen of Bhai Sahib's erudition and charm of style, the book represents the first serious effort to put a philosophical superstructure over the firmly held religious beliefs. The author does not hesitate to cite the works of some of the noted Western thinkers, scientists and psychologists of the early twentieth century, to establish his thesis of the superiority of Sikhism in matters of human deliverance, formation of a humane social order, and the like. The work remained confined to Punjabi readership, as its English translation did not follow.

About two decades before the publication of *Gurmat Nirnay*, Bhai Jodh Singh published his exegetical works, notably commentaries on the Bhagat-Bani and the Japuji.[19] The genius of Bhai Sahib had flourished during the years of the rise and spread of the Sikh renaissance movement known as Singh Sabha, and some of his contemporaries, including Bhai Vir Singh, Principal Teja Singh and Professor Sahib Singh, belonged to the exegetical school called the Singh Sabha Pranali. But Bhai Jodh Singh's name is associated with the traditional school known as Sampardai Pranali.[20] That is so, probably because Bhai Sahib received his training in the Gurbani interpretation under the supervision of Sampardai experts. He followed their methodology in its essentials but introduces some modifications as well. Instead of following their convention of offering several meanings and elaborations of a line or passage, he opts for brevity and one-line one-meaning procedure. According to Dr Taran Singh, Bhai Sahib is conversant with the religious texts and systems of Indian philosophy, but he does not burden his exposition of Gurbani with the knowledge he possesses.[21]

It is the merit of Bhai Jodh Singh's interpretation of the Sikh esoteric literature that in spite of its being literal, it is straight-forward, intelligible and authoritative. More often than not Bhai Sahib appears to be orthodox, even to the extent of being dogmatic, yet he is open-mined to tradition as well as to modernity. References to the classical treatises of Indian philosophy and to modern researches in science and humanities are made by him with equal facility, particularly in his writings such as *Gurmat Nirnay* and Guru Nanak Memorial lectures. With his commanding position in the region of exegetical literature and comparative religion, he essentially remains a theologian of the Sikh faith, and a distinguished one at that.

NOTES

1. Cf. Paul Tillich, *Systematic Theology*, Vol.I, Chicago, 1951, p.26.
2. Panchbati Sandesh, Dehra Dun, April 1982, 'Sikhism' by late Babu Jodh Singh, pp. 6-12.
3. Ibid, p.11.
4. Ibid., p.12.
5. S. Radhakrishnan (ed.), *History of Philosophy; Eastern and Western*, Vol.One, 1952 (1957, 1967), 'Sikh Philosophy' by Bhai Jodh Singh, pp. 515-25.
6. Ibid., p. 519.
7. The Adi-Granth, Var Asa (7.2).
8. A.S.Sethi & R. Pummer (ed.), *Comparative Religion*, New Delhi: Vikas, 1979.
9. History of Philosophy, op.cit.
10. Comparative Religion, op.cit., p.129.
11. History of Philosophy, op.cit., pp 276-7.
12. Comparative Religion, op.cit., p.142.
13. Taran Singh (ed.), *Guru Nanak & Indian Religious Thought*, Patiala: Punjabi University, 1970; (English version by Wazir Singh).
14. Ibid., p.81.
15. Ibid., p.83.
16. Ibid., p.68.
17. Bhai Jodh Singh, *Teachings of Guru Nanak*, New Delhi: G.N.Foundation, 1969,pp.26.
18. Bhai Jodh Singh, *Gurmat Nirnay* (Punjabi), 1932 (reprinted 9 times).
19. Bhai Jodh Singh, Bhagat Bani Steek, 1913 (1957); Japuji Steek, 1980 (revised ed. P.U. Patiala); Bani Bhagat Kair Ji Steek, 1981.
20. Taran Singh, *Gurbani dian Viyakhya Pranalian* (Punjabi), Patiala: Punjabi University, 1980,, p.249-50.
21. Ibid., p.250.

INDEX